*Don't judge yourself by others' standards...
have your own. And don't get caught up
into the trap of changing yourself to fit
the world. The world has to change to fit you.
And if you stick to your principles, values
and morals long enough, it will.*
—Berry Gordy

*The greatest education in the world
is watching the masters at work.*
—Michael Jackson

*You know, you do need mentors, but in the end,
you really just need to believe in yourself.*
—Diana Ross

D1153877

I've been blessed to find people who are smarter than I am, and they help me to execute the vision I have.

—*Russell Simmons*

No matter how hard you work to bring yourself up, there's someone out there working just as hard, to put you down...

—*Dr. Dre*

The thing about hip-hop today is it's smart, it's insightful. The way they can communicate a complex message in a very short space is remarkable.

—*Barack Obama*

Contents

Introduction

L ately, there has been much talk about the declination of urban music such as hip-hop, R&B and reggae due to the lack of concept innovation and content quality. The majority of today's urban musicians, recording artists, and entertainment entrepreneurs compete against each other, lacking sustainable differentiation. Many have argued that a large number of musically talented people and entertainment entrepreneurs have failed to take quality time to scan the music and entertainment business environment in effort to identify and exploit new opportunities. Instead, they energetically pursue success entirely on generating ideas. The ability to generate good ideas is certainly an important skill required for success. However, when it comes down to business, good ideas are not enough. Not every talented musician has the business acumen and analytical skills to identify gaps in a market that could be exploited for profit. Nevertheless, if you have a willingness to learn, the ability to make and carry out personal commitments, and are determined to be successful, then you have what it takes to become an entrepreneur. As a budding musician or entertainment entrepreneur you should not only focus on just generating ideas but on spotting new or neglected opportunities in the music industry and then creating a viable business proposition around the identified opportunity.

Your creative ability to generate good ideas will then assist you with shaping your newfound opportunity to increase your chances of success. Despite the views and opinions of the urban music sector, millions of singles, albums, and videos are still being consumed each day. In fact, as long as human beings remain responsive to the way they feel, i.e. emotionally, music will always be a part of our lives. In regards to music as an industry, given that a musical work has significant relevance, and a legal owner, it will always have the potential to generate income. This is because NO ONE can legally take advantage of that significant relevance in a recorded piece of music unless permission has been otherwise granted.

This book will make clear to independent musical talent and aspiring entrepreneurs the industrious approach in which to take advantage of their skills and abilities, their knowledge and understanding, or other people's resources to establish a viable business by following a series of steps. These include preparing oneself to take the time to scan the music and entertainment markets for superficial gaps and then explore those gaps for possible opportunities. In addition, the undertaker must be completely focused and mentally prepared to take risks and welcome any challenges. The book will also explain the various aspects of the global music industry, provide concepts on entrepreneurship, and make available a comprehensive list of useful music industry contacts.

The number one entity that is driving change in the global music and entertainment industry can be summed up in one word: "broadband." Broadband or "ADSL" is the technology that makes electronic media very fast. Broadband is the reason why most people are now buying music and watching videos from their laptops and iPods. Broadband has changed the way we consume media and enjoy entertainment. This also provides efficiency for entertainment entrepreneurs and musicians who are now able to inexpensively promote their projects to a virtually unlimited number of people free via online venues like YouTube or MySpace. On the downside, music piracy is widespread as the tech industry failed to provide legitimate solutions. Ironically, every problem is an opportunity and this is a huge opening for entertainment entrepreneurs to generate new ideas in effort to seize these undefended opportunities. So, if you're a performance artist, make beats or play instruments, write songs, or have a passion for music and would like to manage, promote talent or publish content, this book is definitely for you.

How to Use This Book

Your goal is to identify new opportunities within the global music and entertainment industry and then produce ideas to seize those opportunities thus creating your own business. At the beginning of this book you will find a detailed report that give analysis of the current conditions of the global music industry up until the next five years, 2015. You are encouraged to fully analyze this report in effort to spot any gaps, issues, openings, requirements or setbacks in the music and entertainment industry in which you can turn into a profitable business opportunity. Once you have studied the industry report, the next stage is to carefully read through each chapter in this book, which have been designed using proven techniques and systematical processes to help you gain the knowledge and understanding of how to successfully generate good ideas to seize opportunities that could then be transformed into a tangible business. The successful reader will establish a resourceful, adaptable, creative, innovative and dynamic sense for building a lucrative business enterprise.

Global Music Industry Report (2010-2015)

Industry Performance

It's no secret that the US music industry has hit hard times. The explosion of the Internet throughout the nation's households has led to a surge in the amount of music both purchased and illegally traded online. Each method of downloading dips into the artists' and their labels' revenue. However, there is a bright spot for record labels amidst the gloom. The global music industry is managing the trend of rapidly falling revenue and profits that is occurring elsewhere in the music business—so much so that revenue is expected to grow by 1.9% annually in the five years to 2010 to $4.9 billion. A booming live performance scene and increasing demands from advertisers are the driving forces behind this growth. Also, the increase in the number of media on which music is available means there are more potential revenue streams if publishing companies are savvy enough to sign effective deals. Where music was once only available on vinyl or cassette, today it is offered on vinyl, CD, DVD, Digital Download, Blu-ray Disc, and more. Even so, 1.9% revenue growth per year is not desirable long term, particularly when other sectors of the industry are on the verge of collapse.

The greatest threat to publishers is the devaluation of music as intellectual property in the face of online downloads. If consumers have access, whether legally or illegally, to artists' intellectual property without going through conventional channels, the value of that intellectual property will likely fall. Also, digital technology is making it easier for artists to get by without a publishing company: they can retain rights to their music and distribute it themselves via applications like iTunes. During 2008 and 2009, the music industry became more vulnerable and certainly more willing to adapt its business model in order to meet consumers' rapidly changing needs. These adjustments have come in the form of innovations and changes, such as moving away from digital rights management (DRM), which puts limitations on the use of digital content, to single-song downloads, releasing interactive applications, launching remix contests, streaming music to phones, and allowing video sites like YouTube to monetize infringement. While demand is set to increase and companies pursue opportunities more vigorously, growth will be slow in the next few years; in fact, revenue only grew 1.4% from 2009 to 2010. But once the economy recovers and popular music becomes even more popular for advertisers, the industry will rebound to about 3.4% average revenue growth per year for the next five years to 2015, totaling $5.8 billion.

Key External Drivers

Industry players are dependent on the protection of intellectual property. Most participants derive revenue from licensing fees. Every time a record is played or a song is performed, the copyright owner must grant permission and issue a license to collect a payment. The more airplay or usage the song receives, the greater the income generated from the song. Take Estelle's "American Boy" or Usher and Will.i.am's "OMG" song; both these songs have received heavy airplay and high usage, and you can only imagine how much income these songs have generated. As measured by US *album sales*, an increase in consumer demand for CDs,

DVDs, LPs and cassettes will lead to an increase in a music publisher's revenue. In addition, an increase in the number of times a song is played or performed will lead to a higher collection of sales revenue. An increase in *spare income* will increase buyers' demand for music products, either online or in CD format.

A commercial airs on television, advertising some ubiquitous product, and a song plays innocuously in the background. It is how much the owners of that song get paid that is central to the performance of the global music industry. And it is already big business—$4.9 billion in 2010—but the most noteworthy aspect of the publishing industry is its resilience during a time when other music sectors are facing near collapse. The global music industry, far more resilient to the digital technology boom than the broader music industry itself, is set to grow about 1.9% per year in the five years to 2010. That said, publishers still face considerable obstacles, similar to those causing drastic reductions in revenue for music production and recording industries. In addition, there is an ongoing debate and cultural change regarding who the actual song owners are.

The Music Industry's Digital Transition

Many revenue streams have been largely unaffected by recent music industry downturns through piracy, and music publishers have benefitted from additional sources of income resulting from the digital exploitation of music in downloads and mobile phone ringtones. There are however, significant obstacles to overcome in the monetizing of digital musical content. The availability of music online and the explosion of available music to advertisers have meant that selling a song is tougher now than in the past. Why would an advertiser pay millions for the rights to the latest hit song by a big name when an equally effective and available song by an unknown artist/group exists? Happy to get the exposure, this artist/group would most likely be willing to lease the rights to the song for a much lower price. In addition, the absence of an international digital infrastructure and consistent international regulation governing digital intellectual property could limit growth potential. Deals must be struck with companies in a different manner across national boundaries; international firms must negotiate different contracts for each region in which they operate. The use of songs in mobile phone products has been one of the most significant digital revenue contributions to music publishers, experiencing very strong growth in the past five years. Revenues from digital downloads and other new products, such as video downloads, have also grown strongly, but they remain quite small but with huge room for growth. And while the use of music specifically for cell phones has been a growth sector, advances in phone technology threaten to make it a redundant product. Faster, cheaper wireless downloading means that whole songs can be downloaded and manipulated on cell phones, potentially making the demand for ringtone-only songs obsolete.

The new glamour product is the video game. The outbreak and popularity of music-oriented games such as *Guitar Hero*, *Rock Band* and *Singstar* have created a huge market for music rights. More importantly, it is a market that artists, game developers, and music labels are keen to exploit: artists can gain much-needed exposure, developers can improve game sales, and labels can increase sales of songs. The use of games to improve back-catalog sales has proven particularly helpful. One of the most important examples that illustrates are the ever-popular Def Jam: Vendetta; Def Jam: Fight For NY; Def Jam: Icon; and the forthcoming Def Jam: Rap Star. Today's artists are growing increasingly independent, which has been a major cause of revenue loss in recent years. As artists gained an understanding of the possibilities of distributing their music online—some artists have elected to do so for no charge, attempting to garner interest in live performances as a revenue earner—there is a growing antagonism toward allowing a record company to retain control of intellectual property, which has led to a drop in revenue.

Protecting Growth Revenue

R esearch has shown that between 2005 and 2010 the global music industry has grown at an average annual rate of 1.9% to $4.9 billion. Thus far, the industry has had few years where revenue has contracted, however, the combination of the ongoing digital music revolution and the parlous state of the US economy is something of a perfect storm, which is expected to lead to a tough year in 2010, with growth of only 1.4%. One of the biggest reasons for the slowdown is a sharp drop in advertising across the nation. Companies, hesitant to invest heavily during times of uncertainty, have been pulling advertisements, reducing the demand for the rights to music. Meanwhile, consumers are less inclined to buy products that contribute to growth, such as sheet music or concert DVDs. Sales of compilation albums, a solid performer of late, are also set to suffer. The industry is continually taking steps to improve enforcement of laws regarding illegal downloading and music sharing online, which should help mitigate losses somewhat. However, this focus on prosecuting those who access music illegally, rather than adapting the industry business model to the new digital environment, has led to artists operating independently or with smaller companies, with strong growth among non-employers, which has resulted in acquisitions by major players attempting to shore up existing revenue.

Performance Revenue

Performance royalties continue to produce significant revenue for the industry. Growing downstream demand for live music performances on stage, in concerts and at other public venues has led to growth in this industry segment. Additionally, broadcasts on the radio and television have consistently supported growth in this segment in the past five years. The distributions of income from the American Society of Composers, Authors and Publishers (ASCAP) and Broadcast Music Inc. (BMI) have gradually increased over the past five years, indicating the growth in the royalties of the performance segment. As more artists attempt to operate independently of record companies, the industry expects performance royalties to find their way directly to artists, rather than publishers. This trend began in 2006, and the effect is unlikely to be severe; it will be the smaller artists, who earn little revenue, who will be the main beneficiaries.

The number of songs and other recordings used in conjunction with advertisements, films, television and other media has been increasing during the current period and is expected to continue growing. However, the value of any given recording has been falling lately as advertisers and producers leverage the Internet to locate appropriate music. This access decreases the chances that a big name will be used, which then lowers the fee amount charged. A notable example of this trend toward sourcing unknown artists is the use of "Are You Gonna Be My Girl" by Jet in an early iPod commercial on TV. Using the song not only generated significant interest in the album and the band, which was relatively unknown in the US, but also allowed the advertiser to gain the license for a price far less than it would have paid for the work of a more popular artist. Profit margins increase as bigger deals are signed; thus, as the industry boomed in the mid-to-late 1990s, profits did too. Between 1998 and 2000, value-added increased by an annualized rate of 10.9%. The rate dropped between 2002 and 2004 to 0.1% as economic growth slowed and lowered advertising expenditure, which caused licensing fees to fall. Average profit is expected to reach an estimated 15.7% across the industry in 2010.

Industry Outlook

The industry's resistance to the digital invasion will persist during the next five years to 2015. In fact, it appears that music licensing will prove resilient to the worst effects of the current recession. By 2015, the industry expects revenue to hit $5.8 billion, an average increase of 3.4% per year. The two significant factors affecting music industries at large, as well as this industry specifically are the current economic downturn and the growing pervasiveness of digital downloads, both legally and illegally. The latter is expected to cause considerable grief for the industry and will be the primary factor driving the slow growth in revenue and wages.

The Digital Threat

Potential growth markets are continually usurped by free services, diminishing an industry's means of generating future income. A notable example is the expectation of deriving royalties from streaming music online; however, websites like MySpace now allow artists to stream a selection of music with no need to pay royalties to anyone.

Increasing independence of artists is another growing concern for the industry. As artists grow more aware of the capacity of the internet to distribute their music to they are less likely to license intellectual property to record companies. The industry expects that music publishers will gain an increasing share of revenue from new opportunities in online music and on cell phones. As CD sales plummet and downloading revenue remained below what CDs once achieved, it was expected that ringtone licensing would be a significant revenue stream. However, research indicates that consumers still prefer purchasing full songs as opposed to ringtones; so mobile purchases are likely to grow as commerce via cell phones grows, while ringtone sales are set to face a sharp decline.

The economic downturn underway in the United States is expected to stall spending on advertising and limit firms' spending on licensing of music for commercial use. This decrease is set to have a greater, but shorter-term, effect on industry growth than digital downloading. After slow revenue growth of 1.4% in 2010, the industry is expected to begin its recovery in 2011, growing by 4.7%. The reason the industry has the potential to grow in the face of poor consumer confidence and a collapsing market for music sales is the ability to use the Internet for music distribution. The growing ubiquity of music to the consumer makes it more useful as a marketing tool. Also, advertisers, marketers and licensers are becoming more aware of what makes music appropriate for advertising.

During the five-year period to 2015, revenue will be affected by a number of other issues, particularly, the change in rate regulations by the government and other influential bodies. The rate-setting process is of vital importance to all music publishers and their songwriters. In 2008, the Copyright Royalty Board (CRB) had to decide whether to set new mechanical royalty rates in the US for the five years from January 1, 2009 to December 31, 2013. The CRB oversees the royalty rates for physical and digital products, including subscription services.

Intellectual Property

Revenue will be affected by the ability to protect intellectual property and the increased use and demand for Internet service and products. The music industry forecasts that the revenue growth will be primarily driven by easier access to global music industry services provided through the mechanical revenue stream, which are per-minute rates set by the government that are paid to the publisher and writer whenever a song or CD is sold. With respect to online use, music publishers are concentrating on the definition and establishment of international, privately driven solutions to provide a global answer for the market in terms of generating royalties through legal digital downloads. When a solution becomes viable, music publishers expect to generate enhanced royalties through the mechanical revenue stream.

The greatest threat posed by digital music's growth is its devaluating effect on music. As consumers access more music at less cost, the value placed on an individual song falls. Despite recent falls in revenue, the industry remains highly profitable, as there are no costs for reproducing content. Once a song is recorded, it can be licensed an infinite number of times to any client willing to pay, limiting production costs and ensuring that popular songs remain profitable for an indefinite time after their release. This trend is beginning to improve profitability in the traditional music business as well.

Small Record Labels

Historically, the publishing sector has been dominated by four record companies: Warner Music, Universal Music, Sony (or Sony BMG), and EMI, mainly due to their foresight in embracing the notion of publishing long ago. Also, and more importantly, the major labels have had access to the vast majority of popular music, which is in much higher demand than more obscure songs. The shift in the delivery of music towards digital delivery and the ease and affordability of digital recording equipment has encouraged a surge in the number of small independent record labels. These labels are often loss-making entities and short-lived, so even though the number of establishments in the industry falls through consolidation by big players, the replenishment by new independents ensures the industry does not become more concen-

trated. In the five years to 2015, the number of large establishments is
set to fall by 1.7% per year, while establishments run by sole proprietors
or partnerships will fall by only 0.1% per year, reaching 1,863. What
this means is that while revenue growth will increase steadily, it will be
centered on major labels that have the networks and capacity to license
their vast libraries of work. The troubles of the music industry at large
will still cause significant difficulties for small labels, and the slow fall in
the number of licensers will continue.

Life Cycle Stage

The job of a music publisher is to link new songs by songwriters with
recording artists to record them, with the intent of generating royalty revenues. Promoting songs, supervising the collection and payment of
royalties, and placing songs in movie soundtracks and commercials allows the development of revenue streams. There are many new revenue
streams available, which will ensure industry viability in the longer term.
As with most firms operating in the information sector of the economy,
companies in this industry now have additional revenue opportunities in
online and mobile music markets. However, these new avenues will also
promote more intense competition between music publishers. Moreover,
the growth in available markets for music publishers—songs being trans-
lated to games, films, television, Internet applications, iPhone applications, and more, suggest an industry that is flourishing. However, the
advent of digital music sharing and downloading technology is beginning to damage the industry. Artists are becoming reluctant to commit
to contracts that relinquish control of their intellectual property. When
retaining control, the need for assistance with promotion and distribu-

tion is less, and can be achieved to a lesser extent by themselves, or an independent label.

These labels often impose less stringent conditions on song ownership than larger firms. The great strength of this industry, and the reason it has avoided sliding into decline, has been the nature of its clients. By licensing music to corporate clients almost exclusively, rather than households, it is far more difficult to lose income through illegal distribution. A song played on radio or in a commercial is easily identifiable, and legal action can be taken for any intellectual property used without permission.

The industry's contribution to GDP has fallen over the past five years, despite strong profits. This has come primarily as revenue growth has been sluggish. Also, an increasing proportion of smaller labels, which may make less profit due to poor economies of scale, have driven down the industry's level of gross product. The industry's profitability forecasts took something of a hit when the Copyright Royalty Board decided against mandating a higher rate of royalties for the use of music. However, 70% of sales from music still go to the record company that owns the track as payment from the retailer for the ownership of the song.

Products and Services

Music publishers earn their revenue from licensing the right to use an artist's songs. Firms in this industry acquire copyrights (or a share of the copyrights) in musical compositions, or enter into agreements to administer copyrights (or a share of copyrights), and exploit the compositions by licensing them for inclusion on records, in television and other media, seeking new uses for the compositions, and administering and collecting the proceeds generated. In return for providing these services, firms are entitled to a percentage of the royalty income, which varies from contract to contract. Music publishing firms derive their revenues from four key sources:

1. Mechanical Royalties

In the USA, mechanical royalties are collected directly by music publishers from recorded music companies or via The Harry Fox Agency, a non-exclusive licensing agent affiliated with the National Music Publishers' Association (NMPA). This is slightly different outside the US, as performing rights organizations and collection societies perform this function. Once mechanical royalties reach the publisher (either directly from record companies or from collection societies), percentages of those royalties are paid to any co-owners of the copyright in the composition and to the writer(s) and composer(s) of the composition. Mechanical royalties are paid at a penny rate of 9.1 cents per song per unit in the US and as a percentage of the wholesale price in most other territories. In the US, these rates are set according to industry negotiations contemplated by the US Copyright Act and are increasing at two-year intervals. For example, through December 2005, firms received 8.5 cents per song and then on January 1, 2006, the rate increased to 9.1 cents per song until December 31, 2007. The rate-setting proceeding is of vital importance to music publishers and their songwriters. The recent, aforementioned Copyright Royalty Board (CRB) decision on mechanical royalty rates, including subscription services, has had a marked effect on forecast performance for the segment. As mentioned, the current statutory rate for both CDs and permanent downloads is 9.1 cents. This is only 7.1 cents above the two-cent rate set nearly a century ago, at the time of the enactment of the compulsory license. Based on the Consumer Price Index, two cents in 1909 would be over 40 cents today, which indicates that this industry may not be experiencing fair royalty rates. Recordings in excess of 5 minutes attract a higher rate. In international markets, multi-year collective bargaining agreements and rate tribunals determine these rates.

2. Performance Royalties

Performance royalties include the broadcast of music on television, radio, cable and satellite, live performance at a concert or other venue (e.g. arena concerts, nightclubs, cabarets). Also included is the broadcasting of music at sporting events, restaurants or bars, online and wireless streaming, and the performance of music in staged theatrical productions. Performance royalties are earned when a song is performed live on stage played in a bar or other public venue or broadcast on the radio or television. Key drivers of growth in this segment are the chart success of songs from rosters of active songwriters and the proliferation of new media channels. Performance royalties are usually collected on behalf of publishers and songwriters by performance rights organizations and collection societies. Key performing rights organizations and collection societies in the US include: The American Society of Composers, Authors and Publishers (ASCAP), SESAC, and Broadcast Music Inc. (BMI). The societies pay a percentage of the performance royalties to the copyright owners (or publishers) and the songwriters of the composition. This segment has grown over the past five years, and the industry expects this to continue, being largely driven by television advertising, live performance and online streaming and advertising royalties.

3. Synchronization Royalties

Synchronization royalties are the industry's white knight. They include the use of music in films or television programs, television commercials, video games, and karaoke machines. In other words, it is the use of the song in combination with visual images. Industry-wide, synchronization revenue has experienced a decade of consecutive year-over-year growth. Publishing firms have been able to drive meaningful growth in synchronization by gaining greater penetration in commercials and video, particularly in the US. Significant licenses have been issued worldwide for a number of major advertising campaigns, TV programs, and video games. Synchronization royalties have experienced strong growth in recent years and will continue to do so, benefitting from the growth of media channels, a recovery in advertising, robust video games sales, and growing DVD sales/rentals. Also, many bands have recently utilized appearances by their music in television programs or advertisements to bolster awareness and album sales. Two notable instances are the band Jet appearing in an iPod ad, and Snow Patrol having its song "Chasing Cars" featured in the closing episode of the hit series "Grey's Anatomy."

4. Other Royalties

"Other" segment revenue typically represents about 8% of industry revenue. Since the absolute amount can vary significantly from year to year, these revenues tend to be irregular and unpredictable. This segment predominantly comprises sheet music, and the publishing of books and films about the creators of music or the songs themselves. Music publishing is the business of acquiring, protecting, administering and exploiting rights in musical compositions. It is a business based on songs owned by the company, as distinct from the recordings, films, commercials or other media that are derived from the songs. Music publishers earn their revenue from licensing the right to use their songs. Firms in this industry acquires copyrights (or a share of the copyrights) in musical compositions, or enter into agreements to administer copyrights (or a share of copyrights), and make use of the compositions by licensing them for inclusion on records, film, television and other media, seeking new uses for the compositions, and administering and collecting the proceeds generated. In return for providing these services, firms are entitled to a percentage of the royalty income, which varies from contract to contract.

Demand Determinants

In order for the owner of intellectual property—in this case, music—to make a profit, the music must be of sufficient quality or public appeal to attract substantial sales which would warrant the licensing of said music to other uses, such as commercials, compilation records, and radio stations. Consumer demand for music is quite naturally correlated to the quality of music available. Also, demand is greater when publicity is widespread or reviews have been good. Firms can generally control the level of advertising they generate; however, reviews are based on artistic merit and the opinion of the reviewer and are therefore less easy to control. The amount of industry-related awards an artist may win (or is nominated for) would positively affect sales. Social, cultural, economic, and demographic factors such as age and changing tastes in music affect demand for certain types of music. Different genres of music appeal to different social, cultural, economic, and demographic groups. Major players in the industry, such as Universal and EMI, have developed techniques—primarily revolving around marketing ploys—to generate interest in music from target markets.

This market-oriented approach to music has shifted the focus of the industry. Whereas once labels would sign and record artists they considered viable, and then promote them, the new client-focused business model demands that the artists produced are what the music-buying public demands. As such, the promotion of "marquee" stars, such as Usher, Black Eyed Peas, and Eminem, and the creation of a fan base, means there is a guaranteed market for music by these artists. Also, record companies can offer incentives to "tastemakers" such as music and teen magazines to print favorable stories, further increasing demand for the music. The level of real household disposable income influences the timing and quantity of musical goods and services purchased from the industry.

The purchase of music is considered a luxury item, and as such, when the level of income declines, households respond by reducing or postponing the purchase of goods (particularly nonessential goods in the musical and entertainment industries). The advent of digital transfer of music online presents positive and negative possibilities for the industry. On one hand, overall demand for music may actually increase, despite the revenue from CD and online sales combined falling over recent years, as more fans access music by artists they were previously unaware of, creating greater opportunities and possibly increasing the value of assets held by the industry. However, as fewer consumers purchase their music legitimately, more direct lines of revenue, such as releasing songs for compilations and radio (which is trending towards 'talk' and away from music broadcasts) means revenue could fall.

Also, as illegal downloads are not publicized it becomes more difficult to identify which music is popular, discouraging companies from investing too heavily in music as a promotional tool. Musical groups often appeal to a special demographic (age, gender, education, income, and marital status being the most important). If the number of people in a certain demographic group increases, then the potential size of the audience for live performances and recorded music increases. As a result, hip-hop artists/groups, who tend to target a younger demographic, will often perform in areas where there is a higher proportion of young people. While the overall demand for music remains unchanged, the value of the license to certain genres can change with demographic shifts.

Major Markets

Large record companies own the majority of industry participants and therefore they work closely with, and offer their music publishing services to, these companies. The largest slice of revenue—36%—comes from the leasing and licensing of intellectual property within and between companies in the industry. Many labels are subsidiaries of the industry's "big four"—EMI, Sony, Warner, and Universal, and rights are often transferred from one to the other. This behavior is likely to continue, but in the interests of cost savings, many firms will limit their charges, lowering the importance of this segment. Compensating for the space created by this is growth in a variety of smaller segments. Industry participants acquire copyrights through the purchase of entire catalogues of music or individual songs. The music is then licensed to record companies, radio, TV, films, commercials, and multimedia applications, in printed or digital form. It is in these segments of the industry that its resilience is founded.

Video games, in particular, are a source of enormous growth, with not only dedicated music games paying big money, but interactive entertainment of all stripes ever-more keen to pay for appropriate songs to enhance their gaming experiences. Beyond this, television and film producers are becoming more aware of the commercial importance of soundtracks to their creations. For example, a television serial aimed at the 15-19 demographic can be well served by including music that appeals to that group. The artists and labels also benefit from this arrangement. Musicians and groups are increasingly attempting to use mass media such as television to reach their target demographic, meaning that they are willing to sell the rights at a lower price than the market may otherwise demand.

Advertisers, too, are happy to increasingly use music to sell products. This is not a new trend, but the success of campaigns that have actively employed music has served as a template for numerous other ad companies. This has, however, created a double-edged sword for publishers. As advertisers (and for that matter TV, film, and game producers) have had greater access to new, previously inaccessible music, they have found useful artists and songs that may be unknown and hence cheaper. In the past, the cachet of well-known artists was a major appeal in using their songs. Today, it is the song, not the artist that is valued. As such, cheap, catchy songs are becoming sought-after and are contributing to a mild softening of revenue growth. Publishers will copyright songs and collect royalties on a worldwide basis. But beyond that, there are no guarantees that songs will succeed. Publishers will attempt to shop for a record deal, pitch material to other artists and place songs in films and TV shows. A publisher will usually offer a one- year deal with an option to renew the artist's contract for up to two more years. Industry sources note that if an author is an unsigned artist, the artist might receive an advance of less than $50,000 for what is called a publishing development deal.

Competitive Landscape

Industry concentration indicates the extent to which major players dominate the industry by such measures as the proportion of industry revenue earned by the four largest industry players, the geographic spread of establishments and the size of company by employee numbers. This industry is classified as having a medium level of concentration. The primary reason for this definition is that we estimate that the industry's four major players—EMI, Vivendi (incorporating BMG and Universal Music Group), Warner Music, and Sony—together generate approximately 60% of industry revenue. According to industry definitions, any industry with major player dominance between 30% and 70% constitutes medium concentration. Concentration in this industry has been subject to recent significant increases, with a number of acquisitions/mergers involving major players. Firstly, Vivendi acquired Universal Music Group, which has since purchased the music arm of Bertelsmann AG (BMG), making Vivendi the industry's largest player. Also, the joint venture between BMG and Sony has created even greater concentration, as these major entities attempt to mitigate a declining market by acquiring smaller, profitable competitors. Major players in this industry tend to own numerous smaller labels, and only sign major names to their labels directly. Over the short to medium term, the industry concentration will increase moderately. This assumption is based largely on the continued aggressive expansion of industry major players, in the face of weak revenue growth.

Five Key Success Factors

There are approximately 250 key success factors for a business within the music industry. The five most important ones are these:

1. **Having a good reputation**
Firms that have a good reputation tend to sign more talented artists who generate greater revenue streams from their performances as well as utilizing their songs in various other royalty segments.

2. **Protection of intellectual property/ copyrighting of output**
Incentives for music publishers to own copyrights for more songs.

3. **Upstream vertical integration: (ownership links)**
Music publishers that have vertically integrated operations have guaranteed access to product promotion and distribution.

4. **Management of a high quality assets portfolio**
Participants ownership of copyrights to songs that are in demand.

5. **Having a wide and expanding product range**
To offer broader product range and capture variations in consumer tastes in music.

Cost Structure Benchmarks

The high rate of return, at around 16.6% of revenue despite a traumatic 2009, indicates the profitability of the global music industry in which an initial purchase or investment can generate revenues over the longer term in the form of royalties. In the breakdown of the market segments, for most co-publishing deals, a music publisher is traditionally paid 50% of the publisher's share of royalty income from the mechanical and synchronization royalty segments. Performance royalty is typically collected by a performing rights organization (BMI, ASCAP, and SESAC being the principle organizations in the US), and a music publisher usually receives 25% of that income. Royalty and copyright costs, manufacturing and distribution costs, marketing and promotion costs, legal, regulatory and consultancy costs, wages, and amortization are the major costs associated with firms.

However, the advent of digital file sharing technology and the ability of artists to deliver new music to listeners via the Internet is removing the need for (prominent) bands and artists to align themselves with big labels, which is likely to hurt profit levels, as big-name acts are the primary source of revenue. Labels will continue to sign young talent as an investment, but young artists will be more aware of the potential associated with the Internet, and will be reluctant to sign long-term contracts, preferring to use the companies' economies of scale to gain assistance in achieving prominence, then attempting to act independently from then on.

Discounting Future Music

At 15.7% of total revenue, amortization accounts for a significant amount of a publishing expense. Songs that may be a hit today will generate significant amounts of royalties; however as time passes the song will be less valuable. Amortization accounts for this drop in value, and firms note that this cost is large. The ephemeral nature of this industry implies that amortization is a significantly larger cost than depreciation, as the product in question is intangible and intellectual in nature. However, amortization may take up a smaller share of revenue in the future, so long as the industry sufficiently embraces digital technology. The ability of consumers to access vast databases of musical information, including songs from any era, at the same place, means that over time the value of a song is less likely to drop as greatly. However, this will be mitigated somewhat by the greater choice available to consumers, which would create downward pressure on the value of songs.

Marketing remains an essential cost to firms, as organizations are involved in many facets of music. From performing concerts, to publishing of music in films, firms must continually promote and market their services, songs, and performers in order to achieve a revenue stream. Music publishers work very closely with integrated record companies to assist with the marketing and promotion of artist records. Research shows that marketing expenses amounted to 20% of revenue for the global music industry. Purchases are a large expense for the global music industry, accounting for 15% of industry revenue. This involves the purchase of existing songs and newly released material as well as other production materials.

Basis of Competition

The industry is very competitive with a large number of firms seeking limited business (i.e. a contract to license popular music, of which there is a discrete amount). Operators in this industry must compete with each other not only to gain contracts with major name artists, but also to license those artists' songs out for as much profit as possible in a highly competitive marketplace.

Internal Competition

Music publishers compete on the range of music compositions held and the characteristics of the recording artists and their music offerings (top-40, hip-hop, rap). Companies compete on the ownership of songs that can achieve public acceptance and are in high demand (over the long-term). Companies also compete for creative talent, both for new artists and those artists who have already established themselves through another producing label. The music industry relies on the exploitation of music talent. The more a company offers an artist in the form of royalties from the use of their songs, the greater the chance that artist Services provided by the publisher are: registering of copyrights, filing information with mechanical and performing rights organizations, auditing record companies and other licensees, bookkeeping, negotiating licenses, checking royalty statements, and collecting monies. The publisher is either attempting to secure a record deal for the author/artist (as an artist) or place the songs with other artists to be recorded on their albums. In this context, the music publisher must have a good brand and/or marketing abilities, particularly networks throughout the industry.

External Competition

External competition exists only insofar as artists are willing to conduct business matters themselves and retain control of their intellectual property. With the advent of digital music downloading, and the increasing capacity of servers to offer downloads directly, the need for musicians to utilize a record company to manage their music is diminishing, and could provide significant competition in the future. Music competes with other forms of entertainment in a general sense, but when it comes to the use of music and how it is licensed, that competition is diminished, as, for example, a radio station is unlikely to license a film or television program to advertise itself.

Barriers to Entry

The moderate barriers to entering this industry reflect the low level of capital investment needed to start in business, including the reasonable costs of acquiring profitable artists. The industry is based largely on personality—an extensive network of contacts is essential both as means of winning clients and as a way of on-selling licensed music for a profit to a variety of media. Many smaller establishments operate with only a handful of clients and take a 50% cut on most work licensed. Larger firms have extensive rosters of clients, often those who are also subject to recording contracts (control of intellectual property is often a condition in any recording contract), and utilize economies of scale to maintain existing clients and attract new clients who offer potential future returns.

The number and height of barriers to entry is falling slowly. This is due primarily to the advent of digital technology empowering artists more than ever before. Artists in musical industries, given greater control over their own products, will often be inclined to ally with smaller and/or independent labels in order to retain creative control, as the distribution of music becomes easier.

However, there still remain prominent barriers to entry. The five major players in this industry are EMI Group, Warner/ Chappell, BMG Music Publishing, Universal Music Group, and Sony/ATV Music Publishing. Together these five companies account for more than 50% of industry revenue. The five majors all have strong brand recognition. As a result, talented artists tend to prefer to approach well-established and reputable companies. Also, delivering a product or service synonymous with a superior or consistently good product or service from competing organizations is a significant barrier to entry. Having the resources, scale, reputation and potential to integrate vertically helps firms to achieve higher margins and dominance among players. Firms able to record, produce, distribute and publish music will succeed in winning artists as they can perform all the steps needed in the recording industry. In many industries a copyright/patent is important in leading to much higher margins than otherwise would apply. Industry players are dependent on the protection of intellectual property through copyright protection laws. Patent protection can be a costly exercise, particularly for those uneducated on such matters.

Industry Globalization

Warner Music, a division of Warner Brothers, is one of the industry's largest players, operates in numerous international markets, primarily European and Australian, but increasingly in the growing South American market. The declining nature of the music industry in developed nations means that US players are increasingly looking to buffer earnings by branching into such markets, which have lower Internet penetration, and hence are ironically less likely to be experiencing the same technology-prompted slowdown. Consolidation is increasing in this industry. Mergers and acquisitions are attempted regularly, which is not constrained within the US. Many opportunities are being sought after overseas, therefore firms are growing on a global scale. Analysis indicates that this industry has a high level of globalization because many participants are owned by overseas parent companies such as Sony (Japan), BMG (German), EMI (UK) and Vivendi Universal (French) who have major offices in the US as well as internationally.

Increasing use of Internet technology is substantially affecting the industry's revenue-earning capability, as freely available music online (whether legally or not) is devaluing the rights held to music by publishing companies. Also, the ability of musicians to release music internationally, and of publishers to license its use overseas is increasing the industry's global reach. The global music industry's level of globalization is expected to increase in the future. While the industry is dominated by multinationals, music is licensed to record production companies, radio, TV, films, in printed or digital form throughout the world. As the bulk of major players in the industry are already internationally owned, any key acquisitions will be likely to increase the industry's level of globalization into the future.

Major Industry Players

Vivendi Plc

Vivendi is a French based global communications and entertainment giant. It is involved in a number of businesses through its operating segments including telecommunications, television, mobile telephones, video game publishing and music publishing. Vivendi's involvement in the music publishing is through its wholly owned Universal Music Group

(UMG). Universal Music Group (UMG) was purchased by the French media group Vivendi in 2000 and is currently the largest music company in the world. UMG produces, markets, and distributes recorded music throughout the world in all major music genres. The company also manufactures, sells and distributes video products in the US and internationally, and has a network of subsidiaries, joint ventures and licensees in 75 countries. UMG manages around 14 major recording labels and holds an estimated 25.6% global market share of the physical music market (slightly higher for the digital market). UMG holds the strongest position in the recorded music business, particularly in the North American and European markets, which together account for nearly three quarters of global sales. In 2007, the company, through Universal Music Group, received approval for its acquisition BMG Music Publishing in a deal valued at EUR 1.63 billion. This created a new leader within the global music industry and brought the combined market share to its present level. UMG's music publishing segment is projected to record annualized revenue growth of 13.0% between 2006 and 2010.

The bulk of this growth occurred early in the timeframe, driven by the acquisition of BMG's publishing arm. The annual variations are also distorted by decreases in the relative values of the US dollar to the Euro, which appreciated through 2008 but took a steep downturn in 2009 and early 2010. This explains the decline in 2009, as the company's revenue and EBITDA increased in Euro denominated terms. Other than the impact of exchange rates, the publishing segments earnings and margins have been extremely steady. Growth or declines are typically attributable to acquisitions of new contracts or divestitures.

EMI Group Plc

EMI Group, a UK-based music company, is facing severe challenges from the new media environment. In financial year 2006/2007, the company reported a loss of around US$400 million, and a revenue drop of 16% globally and of 13% in the US. This led to its sale to Terra Firma Capital Partners, a private equity firm. The loss of several key artists from the roster before and after the reported loss caused and exacerbated EMI's difficulties. Terra Firma have since announced that cost-cutting procedures will be implemented with the intention of reducing staff by 1,500 people, and overall costs by around US$380 million. The sale had little impact in improving the company's fortunes in 2008, as another loss was recorded. However, even though licensing revenue fell, its importance to the company has soared. Music publishing revenue decreased by 12.3%, as EMI managed to continue to derive revenue from existing licensing agreements, whereas new revenue in music production and sales requires new music to be produced and purchased, and this is where the industry is experiencing difficulties. Over the past three years, licensing and publishing has gone from representing less than 20% of revenue to more than 30%—a clear indication of the state of the industry at large.

In summer 2006 EMI announced it had abandoned its plans for a Warner Music Group deal. In 2007, the company's revenue fell by around 15.8% to $3.43 billion, primarily due to losing major artists that once would have contributed considerable revenue. EMI's publishing operations are less profitable than other major labels, primarily as the largest acts on the label, such as the Beatles, have rights co-owned with other entities, in this case Apple Records. In 2006 EMI once again offered a bid for Warner Music Group, this time for $4.2 billion, however the bid was again rejected. Warner Music Group subsequently made a $4.6 billion counter-bid for EMI, which EMI also rejected. As mentioned, EMI and Warner have tried to combine operations previously, but European regulators prevented efforts.

In 2010, the company teetered on the brink of insolvency. The company was unable to strike licensing deals with other giants within this industry to distribute and market its music in the US. EMI asked for cash payments in exchange for distribution rights in the US to improve its liquidity and secure additional financing. In the now-likely scenario that EMI does fold, Citigroup, its lender, would take control of the label and possibly break it up or sell it off EMI's publishing sector generates more than twice as great a share of company profit as it does overall revenue. This is predominantly due to the low cost nature of the industry segment. The recording and distribution of music requires significant investment in physical media (i.e. CDs), logistics (i.e. transport) or capital (i.e. recording equipment), while licensing of music rights incurs far lower costs.

Warner Music Group Plc

In May 2005, Warner Music Group (WMG) became the only stand-alone music company in the United States. The year before, Time Warner had sold WMG to a group of private investors including Thomas H. Lee Partners, Edgar Bronfman Jr., Bain Capital, and Providence Equity Partners for around $2.6 billion.

WMG remains a global music company, which operates in more than 70 countries through a range of subsidiaries, affiliates and licensees. Warner is one of the world's major music content companies, and is composed of two businesses: Recorded Music and Music Publishing. The company's Music Publishing segment operates internationally. The company earned 41% of its publishing revenue within the US during 2009, up from 36% in 2008.

The decline in revenue was primarily related to a slide in mechanical revenues of $33 million and performance revenue of $17 million. This is consistent with the broader industry's shift away from physical sales and a downturn related decline in spending. This was partially offset by a $14 million increase in digital sales, a trend that is projected to continue in the coming years. Such a shift would have a favorable impact on profitability as digital sales have a lower marginal cost. Additionally, segment level revenues were hindered by a strengthening of the US dollar, which led to a decrease in the value of international sales.

Sony Corporation of America

Sony/ATV Music Publishing is a business segment of Sony Corporation of America and is a joint venture between Sony Corporation of America and Michael Jackson and his estate. Sony/ATV has offices in 40 countries around the world and owns and administers the rights to titles from a broad range of artists (more than 400,000 songs) including Beyoncé, Usher, Destiny's Child, and Bob Dylan. Sony/ATV has the largest country music catalog (after purchasing the Acuff-Rose country music catalog from Gaylord Entertainment for $157 million consisting of 55,000 compositions including the songs of Hank Williams, Roy Orbison, The Everly Brothers, and Felice & Boudleux Bryant, among many others) and also owns more than 250 of the Beatles' songs.

Sony/ATV licenses its songs for use in movies, television, and advertising and collects royalties for its songwriters. In August 2004, Sony BMG Music Entertainment was created through a global 50/50 joint venture between Sony Corporation of America and Bertelsmann AG. Sony has seen rapidly falling revenue across its music production and distribution networks over recent years, however, it has maintained solid growth in publishing, and retains market share of around 7%, with revenue of around $330 million. Sony BMG, a 50-50 joint venture with Bertelsmann AG's Music Group (aka BMG)—recently acquired by Universal Music Group, which is itself a division of Vivendi—in August 2004, and currently generates approximately $400 million annually for both owners combined. However, with the purchase of BMG by Universal, a division of market leader Vivendi, the Sony BMG joint venture was abandoned, as Sony purchased BMG's share of the company. However, Universal Music (Vivendi) purchased the company's publishing rights in 2006, substantially devaluing Sony's share of the segment.

Others

Most industry players are subsidiaries of large music companies such as Sony Music Entertainment, BMG Entertainment, EMI Music Group, Universal Music Group, and Warner/Chappell Music Group. Operating in an industry with a medium level of industry concentration, the top four major players in this industry account for between 49% and 58% of the market share.

In September 2006, it was announced that Universal had agreed to acquire BMG Music Publishing Group from Bertelsmann. The acquisition has been approved by US and EU merger authorities and represents the formation of the largest music publishing company with a share of global revenues potentially in excess of 25%, making Universal both the largest recorded music company and music publishing company. The music publishing business is highly competitive. The five major players identified in the Major Player section of this report collectively account for around 58% of the US market. EMI Music Publishing and WMG

(Warner/Chappell) are the market leaders in music publishing, holding maximum estimates of 20% and 16% shares of the market, respectively. They are followed by BMG at around 12%, Universal at around 10% and Sony/ATV Music Publishing at around 5%.

Technology and Legal Conditions

The main technological advancement used by the global music industry has been the introduction of the Internet. The Internet has allowed for music publishers to perform business online. There are more than 230 legal online music stores throughout the world (EMI Annual Report, 2007). Estimates are that by 2011, digital downloads will comprise over one quarter of all music sales in the industry, and that there are already hundreds of millions of illegal downloads each month, something that has continued to grow despite constant efforts to prevent it by major music companies. This increase in illegal access to music is verified by falling sales figures, in dollar value, if not in volume, even when including digital downloads. While this will not directly affect publishing revenues, easier access to music, and a devalued music industry, is likely to diminish the fees that can be charged to use music as intellectual property, as there will likely be more music available freely.

Furthermore, the increased freedom made available by this technology is likely to embolden numerous artists into avoiding contracts with major labels, and retaining rights to their own work, as British band Radiohead did in October 2007, when they released a record entirely via their own website, bypassing record companies, and retaining control and revenue from their work.

Many participants have developed online systems that authorize the sale of music over the Internet. For example, some industry participants have a music search engine on their website which allows for individuals to search and listen to any song held by the publishers. An online request form for a license from the music publisher can be filled out and submitted once a particular song is chosen and the transaction can be completed over the Internet. The Internet has increased accessibility to music publisher services and has positively impacted the industry.

Regulations and Policy

The global music industry is dependent on the protection of copyrights and is therefore highly regulated. Federal, state, digital music, and international laws affect this industry.

- The Fair Use Doctrine, a Federal law, limits the extent to which a citizen may use a quote from copyrighted material depending on the nature of the use (commercial purpose, nonprofit, educational).

- The Sonny Bono Copyright Term Extension Act extends US copyright from the life of the author plus 50 years, to life of the author plus 70 years.

- State antipiracy laws protect against unauthorized duplication making it illegal to copy, reproduce, and distribute songs without authorization.

Digital Music Laws

- The Digital Performance Right in Sound Recordings Act of 1995 (DPRA) allows copyright owners of sound recordings the right to authorize certain digital transmissions of their works. As amended in 1998, the Digital Millennium Copyright Act (DMCA) covers cable and satellite digital audio services, webmasters, and future forms of digital transmission. The DMCA prohibits the manufacture and distribution of services designed for the sole purpose of undermining technology used to protect copyrighted works.

- The No Electronic Theft Law (NET Act) allows individuals suspected of sound recording infringements to be criminally prosecuted even where no monetary profit or commercial gain is derived from the activity.

CHAPTER ONE

Having The Right Mindset

*"Whatever the mind can conceive
and believe, it can achieve."*

—Napoleon Hill

Mental Preparation

"Good luck is a residue of preparation."

—Jack Youngblood

E very accomplished entrepreneur will agree that mental preparation is essential for new venture creation. In order to truly be effective as an entrepreneur, you must be constantly shaping the way you think to avoid wasting time and money on flawed opportunities.

The quotation "Whatever the mind can conceive and believe, it can achieve." from writer Napoleon Hill, conveys an extremely powerful message. It suggests that you must totally believe in your dreams and abilities with a burning passion and if you do so, it will happen. This is how many successful musicians and entertainment entrepreneurs started. They thought of something, sometimes innovative or sometimes imitative, and started to believe that they could make it work, backing this belief with a burning desire to make it happen. Today, the music industry has an extremely competitive environment, where to become a winner or to successfully create, build and maintain a music business one must have the correct mindset with 100% determination.

Understanding how mind power works will enable you to retain a clear psyche to set in motion skills to harness the astonishing powers of self-belief and determination. Determination could be described as the act by which a person or group of people make up their mind to do or achieve something. Nobody is ready for anything unless they believe they can accomplish it. In other words, if you have a feeling that it might not work or happen, then it will not work or happen. In order to make it work you *need* to have a state of mind that *believes* things will happen and not a state of mind that hopes or whishes for things to happen. It has been proven by many successful music entrepreneurs that having faith and a desire to achieve will immediately eliminate failure. In fact, having a desire to succeed is all you need. Faith could be described as a state of mind encouraged by repeated instructions to the subconscious psyche. Your faith is the key element that determines the actions of your subconscious mind, So for example, saying things like "I truly believe that I am capable of selling 10,000 MP3s on the Internet for 85¢ ($8,500) within the next six months" is an affirmation that will transmute into a reality via the power of self belief and faith, but that is *only* if you truly *believe* this could happen and not that you wish or want it to happen.

Take, for example, Sean Combs, aka P. Diddy. We already know that Diddy is an extremely intelligent man who gained entry to Howard University and accomplished top marks for his academic endeavours. However, the real story begins with his burning desire to enter the music industry. He always had dreams to source and manage talent and believed that if he started out as an intern, he could prove himself. Combs worked relentlessly as an unpaid intern, and eventually rose to be the director of A&R of Uptown Records at the age of 23, where he signed acts such as Mary J. Blige, Total, and Jodeci, bringing the label pure profit with mind-blowing record sales. Sadly, a professionally threatened Andre Harrell, CEO of Uptown Records, fired Diddy, saying, "There cannot be two lions in the jungle." But this was a clear opportunity for Diddy to pursue his ambition to create his own record company and he did. He created Bad Boy Records, signing both Craig Mack and The Notorious B.I.G.

So, for all you up and coming entrepreneurs, never forget that under every problem lays an opportunity, and that every opportunity requires creative ideas in order to seize and establish a viable business proposition.

"If you dream and you believe, you can do it."

—P.Diddy

The Power of Focus

"My success, part of it certainly, is that I have focused in on a few things."

—Bill Gates

Nothing can be achieved in business without seriously concentrating on the task in hand. The brain is an amazing power station that could power a whole city if utilized properly. Every successful entrepreneur will tell you that the main setback to achieving success is the inability to focus on just *one* task at a time and follow it through to its completion. Regardless of who you are, you can still achieve what ever it is you desire by learning how to focus on a single task or goal at a time. This method is often referred to as "small successes," where the completion of each goal is a small success.

It is a scientific fact that wherever we place our focus, the rest of our mind and emotions follow. So by channeling this power, we are able to achieve whatever we believe. As a budding entrepreneur looking to enter the music industry, your key task before any business planning should be to focus on niche markets within the music industry then identify any opportunities that has been neglected by established businesses. A good example of a hip-hop entrepreneur benefiting from the Power of Focus is the founder of Murder Inc Records (now known as The Inc) Mr. Irv Gotti. Irv identified a gap in the R&B sector of the music industry, where he believed he could hold down a share of the market with a hot flagship artist.

Irv Gotti discovered the outstanding Ashanti and generated profitable ideas to break her to the commercial audience. He believed that she had the potential to reach millions of fans across the world. Having identified this opportunity, Gotti immersed himself in the studio for weeks on end until he was satisfied that he had the right selection of songs to make a career for Ashanti. This isolation from others enabled him to focus 100% on making Ashanti's debut album. He was confident about the opportunity and believed he had the potential to make it happen. The outcome? Ashanti's debut album *Ashanti* sold over 500,000 copies in its first week of release in the USA in April 2002. Ashanti went onto break numerous records, and has sold 23 million albums worldwide, and is a bona fide star in the music industry. So remember, always focus on your potential and not on your limitations.

The Law of Attraction

"Whether you think you can or can't either way you are right."
—*Henry Ford*

The Law of Attraction is a universal law that empowers us to create our own realities. The theory suggests that through our very own thoughts and feelings, we attract things we want and don't want. We attract the people and relationships in our lives, and even the cash in our pockets. Basically, if you believe that you lack the ability to successfully create and maintain a business, you will attract limited success and compromise any growth for your business. On the other hand, if you believe anything is possible, and sky's the limit, phenomenally, your positive thoughts will allow you to break through any barriers to entry. Whatever you're thinking on the inside the majority of the time will replicate itself on the outside.

Wiley is an exemplar student of this thought. Simply, Wiley is the King of the UK underground music scene and is also referred to as the Godfather of Grime by fans in Europe. Wiley has a strong musical background and a consistent catalogue of music that is on par with any of the top USA hip-hop artists. But the main reason why Wiley is a perfect example of how the Law of Attraction could help you to attain success in the music industry, is the fact that Wiley has been involved in nurturing and developing talent from London to successfully break the commercial music world. You name them, and it's likely that Wiley was involved somewhere. From the likes of Tinchy Stryder, Jammer, Chipmunk, Doctor, Ice Kid, Kano, JME, Skepta, Roll Deep, and most famously Dizzee Rascal, Wiley has mentored, nurtured and developed them. If he hasn't been directly involved, then he has influenced them to make their mark on the UK music scene. This shows that Wiley has a burning passion for the UK underground music scene, and desires to bring it to the forefront of the global music scene. Wiley attracts the best talent, and in turn helps them make the best of themselves. The law of attraction states that you will start to attract what you believe in, and Wiley personifies that as he believes that people are at their most creative when they are youthful and do things to spark interest and controversy. Wiley has, and will continue to attract Britain's best urban talent in order to keep the British entertainment scene innovative, fresh and dynamic.

The Law Of Attraction theory has a creative process and includes three core elements in which to generate actual success.

These are as follows:

YOU MUST KNOW EXACTLY WHAT YOU WANT AND WRITE IT DOWN. INCLUDE ANY DATES, FIGURES AND DESIRED OUTCOMES.

YOU MUST HAVE TOTAL BELIEF IN WHAT YOU WANT AND PROVIDE AS MUCH ENERGY AS POSSIBLE TOWARDS IT.

YOU MUST STAY FOCUSED, CONFIDENT AND READY TO SEIZE ANY OPPORTUNITIES IN ORDER TO RECEIVE YOUR DESIRED OUTCOMES.

Time Management

"All great achievements require time."

—David Schwartz

Time management is important for every entrepreneur starting or running a business. Managing work with your personal life requires a special type of time management. In order to succeed with your new venture you will *need* to produce a time management program and follow it through religiously as self-discipline is the key driver for victory. Time management itself is the process of arranging, organizing, scheduling, and budgeting your time for the purpose of efficient and measurable progress. However, time management is not exclusively about getting loads of things done, it's also about making sure that you are working on the *right* and *important things*. This aim is to accomplish a lot more in less time, whilst feeling more relaxed, focused and in control of your life. If you don't create a system to manage your time well, it could lead to less productive results and a lacking ability to get things done.

Below are a few important tips on how you could go about managing one of your most valuable and scarce resources (time) for success.

WRITE OR RECORD EVERYTHING DOWN

Never make the mistake of leaving everything to memory. This will lead to information overload. Stick it down on paper or type it up on a word processor. Alternatively, most mobile phones have functions where you could record your ideas and back them up on a PC. If you are a person who often generates great ideas spontaneously then it might be a good idea to invest in a dedicated digital voice recorder.

PRIORITIZING

Time management works a treat when a rating system is applied. The ABCD analysis is one of the most effective systems for prioritizing. Many successful entrepreneurs have deployed it to sort out the most important things against the less important things. So for example the important things to get done will go in the "A" section and the less important things in the "B" section and so on.

SEVEN-DAY ACTION PLAN

Spend at least 1 hour every Monday morning to plan a weekly schedule. First write down your aims or what it is exactly you would like to accomplish by the end of the week. Doing this would help increase your productivity as well as provide a healthy balance between your business and personal life.

THINK BEFORE YOU COMMIT

You do not want to overload yourself with too much work or activities that require quality time. Before committing to a new task stop and think about what is required of you, ask yourself questions such as, "Do I have the time to do this? Will doing this help me achieve my core goals?" If you truly believe that you can undertake the new task without compromising on your other objectives then go for it, if you can't, just say NO.

PERSONAL DEVELOPMENT AND LEARNING

It is extremely important to put a side some time in your seven-day schedule to learn new things and develop your skills and talents. A good example is to enroll on an evening course in business finance or taxes, you could even read books or watch online documentaries.

IDENTIFY YOUR BAD HABITS

The key is to make a list of all the bad habits that hold up your time, sabotage your goals and block you from moving towards success. Bad habits can be easily replaced with good habits. You must identify exactly what things threaten your chances to success and then eliminate them.

Now that you have gained an understanding behind the importance of getting your mind right for creating a new business venture, how to prepare a seven day time management schedule to get things done and have a clear metal picture of your desired outcomes, you are or should be unstoppable, that is unless you allow yourself to procrastinate. Many up-and-coming entrepreneurs have the potential to make millions but fail to do so due to procrastination. According to Napoleon Hill, in his book "Think and Grow Rich," procrastination is the most common cause of business failure. He mentions the fact that numerous people with talents and abilities often miss out on golden opportunities simply because they believe that they need to wait for the time to be right before they start doing what they dream of doing. This is procrastinating, the act of putting things off. The truth is there is never a right time, so start working straightaway. Never wait for a right moment just start now. Work with whatever tools and resources you have, your energy and faith will provide you with the solutions for your success.

CHAPTER TWO

Scanning For New Opportunities

*"Business propositions are born
to opportunities."*

—*Cosmo Anderson*

Entrepreneurship

"The only place where success comes before work is in the dictionary."

—Vidal Sassoon

The concept of pursuing moneymaking opportunities without being constrained by insufficient resources has always been a challenging mission for enterprising people. The mission requires many factors to actually bring about real success. Managing those factors is usually the most important part of the progression. The management process is known as "entrepreneurship" and the undertaker is referred to as the "entrepreneur." Ultimately, entrepreneurship is being able to discover, pursue, and seize the value from business opportunities.

With the rise of the digital age, becoming a successful entrepreneur within the music industry requires effective observations, rigorous research, and a sound business proposition. It is your task to bridge the gap between creativity and the marketplace. You must also be prepared to take risks with your own time and money whilst focusing heavily on delivering products and services that will change or add value to people's lives. The goal for all you up-and-coming entrepreneurs is to stay attuned to opportunity whilst constantly aiming to do things differently from and better than others. The music and entertainment industry is filled with opportunities and has plenty of room for innovation. Your role as the entrepreneur consists of bringing people, money, ideas, and resources together in effort to create value in the music industry. Most successful music and entertainment entrepreneurs all know that skill is just knowledge demonstrated by action. In other words, it's an ability to perform in an effective way.

Damon Dash, co-founder of Roc-a-Fella Records, is an excellent example of somebody who undertakes the pursuit of opportunity without being constrained to limited resources—a true entrepreneur. Despite the recent allegations in the media on Dame being penniless and desperate, through Roc-a-Fella we witnessed the business-savvy and entrepreneurial nature of Dame Dash. Possibly one of the most ambitious entrepreneurs the global music industry has ever seen in the post-Motown Records era, he grew up in East Harlem, known to many as an enterprising person, someone with vision and the ability to generate lucrative ideas as well as having the ability to influence the people around him. In the early 1990s Dash was a club promoter, hosting his own parties using the profits to establish a new music management company. Damon went on to sign Brooklyn native Shawn "Jay-Z" Carter, a talented rapper who had been previously turned down by other record companies. Dash's approach to establishing his newly signed recording artist was totally entrepreneurial. Along with Jay-Z and Kareem "Biggs" Burke, without regard to limited resources he committed to the opportunity to create Roc-a-Fella Records, with Priority Records as the distributing company. From their progress and small successes of their projects, Roc-a-Fella Records attracted several business opportunities, one of which was a signing with the legendary Island Def Jam Recording Company for $5 million in 1997. Just a few years later, the "Roc" became a cultural movement that inspired millions of people across the world. The Company grew into becoming a lifestyle brand selling millions of albums globally. By the late 1990s Roc-a-Fella's annual revenue had surpassed $50 million. This gave Dash the prominence and power to seize new opportunities in adjacent markets. Everybody knows that Damon Dash was the driving force behind the "Roc" using Jay-Z's desire to be the most successful rapper as the "product." Dame was extremely insightful and had the ability to generate lucrative ideas by using his ability to control other people's resources to make things happen. Like all visionary entrepreneurs, Dame identified the opportunity to apply the brand to several other markets, which included the footwear, apparel, and film industries. He realized that since the majority of his target audience spent significant amounts of money on drinking in nightclubs, he could create a business serving them a trendy spin on vodka, therefore making his mark in the alcoholic drinks industry. This type of entrepreneurial activity had never been seen before in the hip-hop culture. It goes without saying, music endorsements and sponsorships had always been around but nothing like what the enterprising Dame Dash, the management guru Kareem "Biggs" Burke, and the ambitious rapper Jay-Z had accomplished.

"The people that I was helping, once they realized their dreams, they did what a criminal would do. They stabbed you in the back. Think about the frustration of building a brand for years that should be taking care of your family, and then the person that was the closest to you saying, 'Nah, you can't have no parts of it,' and flushing it."

—Dame Dash

So, do you think you have what it takes to be a successful entrepreneur in the music industry? Are you ready to share your profits and copyright ownership? Are you ready to turn your talents, skills, and passion into a thriving business? Or will you learn new skills to increase your chances for success? Below is a series of questions that will verify if you are ready to become a successful entrepreneur in today's entertainment industry.

- Do you have a clear vision of where you want to be in five years?

- Do you honestly believe you have something valuable to offer?

- Do you consider yourself to be a self-starter?

- Would you say that you are a good decision maker?

- Do you understand why research is important for your success?

- Are you able to tolerate high levels of risk?

- Do you have any of your own money to invest in the business?

- Can you commit yourself fully to building a new business?

- Are you able to influence and motivate others?

- Can you read financial statements?

- Are you willing to learn new skills and theory?

- How will you react if your business partner became greedy and disloyal?

How to Identify New Opportunities

"Opportunities multiply as they are seized."

—Sun Tzu

Entrepreneurs are people who discover and take advantage of new opportunities. Business opportunities never present themselves. It is the job of the entrepreneur to constantly scan the window for opportunities. Business opportunities could be described as unexploited chances to do something different or better than it is currently being done. Key areas in which you could seek to exploit are listed below:

- New products: exploiting new technology to create new products

- New services: a new or better way to undertake a particular task or problem

- New production techniques: a new or better way of making something

- New distribution methods: a new or better way to deliver products

Business opportunities are often vague and elusive due to the fact that it is very difficult to make out the good ones from the bad ones. Whether your goal is to rule the creative or the performance side of the music industry or provide services behind the scenes, a value proposition must be present. The most difficult job music entrepreneurs face is determining if the business idea is doable and if it offers any value proposition. The best way to verify this is by formulating a scheduled plan to assist you to conduct a thorough investigation into the business idea or opportunity. This is known as "opportunity analysis."

Opportunity analysis will provide you with the detailed facts on the prospects of your business idea by answering questions such as, "Is this business idea viable? How big is the opportunity? Should I continue to pursue this idea or shall I do something else?" Ultimately your goal would be to outline the factors that would make your business idea a success. Most people when they first hit upon a new business idea rush headlong into action only to stumble at the first barrier. Before rushing headlong into investing time and money into your new business idea, it is important that you give yourself time to explore the best available opportunity.

It is very important that you attain up-to-date knowledge of your market, be aware of any gaps, and any problems or industry issues, and that you have a clear understanding of what influences or motivates the customers in your particular marketplace (e.g. Hip Hop, R&B). It is best practice to give yourself time to develop alternatives. The more alternative views you have on a business opportunity, the greater it is to generate viable ideas for a business proposition. Business opportunities and business ideas are completely separate from each other. You need to first identify an opportunity or a problem before generating ideas or a solution that will offer your chosen marketplace a sound business proposition. Plenty of would-be music entrepreneurs do have the ability to produce good ideas. However, they never get the success they anticipated, or if they do get to make it happen, it flops. Why? Before using their abilities to generate good ideas, they fail to search for open business opportunities.

They spend all their time and money on their ideas only to find that the consumers (people who buy) do not need or want what they are offering. It is crucial that you do not forget that spending quality time on identifying what people need or want (opportunities) is just as important, if not more important, than generating good and creative ideas or solutions.

There are many individuals who go around calling themselves entrepreneurs due to the fact they are gifted in coming up with nice ideas. However, the role of an entrepreneur is not to be an ideas person but to have an ability to build a viable business around an opportunity. The same goes for musicians. Good songwriters and rappers always develop their ideas by watching other people's lives, or even their own as a source of inspiration. In addition, having a memorable hook brings the whole ideology together. Unfortunately, the music industry has its own graveyard filled with tombstones that commemorate millions of superficial songs and ventures that had not been developed appropriately in order to accomplish success.

If you don't follow a systematical procedure then your projects will end up in the graveyard too. Whether it's a new business, a song, or a rap, always start the process of creating something by defining or reframing the opportunity. Once you're certain that you are on to something, that's when you start generating creative ideas.

Below is a series of useful pointers to help you look for opportunities in the music industry:

- Never get emotionally attached to a business idea. Detachment and remoteness helps.

- Always try to rise above a "that-will-do" attitude. Always search for alternatives.

- Never seek to start a business on just a good idea. Search for opportunities first.

- Avoid trying to implement your first idea. All ideas have the ability to be developed.

- Always keep an open mind. This is important for the creative process.

- Forget about becoming a "me-too" entrepreneur or musician. Be innovative.

- Gather facts, clues and evidence. Get your detective game on. Ignorance is expensive.

- Always ask yourself questions. Forget assumptions. Challenge everything

- Don't be afraid to abandon your ideas for new ones. It's all part of the game.

- Include your gut feelings when making decisions. Intuition is important.

- A *"eureka* moment" is just a myth. Seek for real business opportunities.

- There are NO right or wrong answers. Just what's best for you.

- Questionnaires, surveys, and interviews are excellent ways to identify opportunities.

- Explore and challenge your initial understanding of an opportunity

How to Generate Good Ideas

"The way to get good ideas is to get lots of ideas and throw the bad ones away."

—Linus Pauling

Where do good ideas come from? How would you know if your idea is viable or worth investing in? Good ideas spring into the world from a central source, a source of inspiration that enables us as humans to generate thoughts that seek to solve problems. Every idea is a new discovery and in some instances can be life changing. Noble Prize-winner George Bernard Shaw said, "If you have an apple and I have an apple and we exchange these apples then you and I will still each have one apple. But if you have an idea and I have an idea and we exchange these ideas, then each of us will have two ideas." This is a great analogy, which sums up the uniqueness of an idea. So where exactly do ideas come from? The generation of ideas may arrive from numerous sources, which may include:

- A divine quality
- Serendipitous activity
- Planned luck
- Endurance
- Methods

Creativity is driven by inspiration, and ideas are the results of that in-spiration. So hypothetically speaking, in order to generate creative ideas one must acquire a source of *inspiration*. Inspiration is often affiliated with vision or genius and is synonymous with influence. Inspiration could come from anywhere it could come from past experiences, rela-tionships, pain, and anger. However, it all depends on the individual and the circumstances. People are inspired in different ways. A musician may get his or her inspiration from weird sounds or noises from things like a washing machine. This could inspire him or her to generate crea-tive ideas. The personal background of the inspired individual is critical to the creative outcomes.

There are numerous techniques to help you shape, challenge, and over-turn your original ideas. Your original ideas are just the first piece of the jigsaw puzzle. If you want to make the most of your ideas, in terms of success, then it is best to approach developing your ideas using both convergent and divergent techniques. The broad term for this approach is known as "Whole Brain Thinking." This approach enables you to de-velop new perspectives on your initial idea using both intuition and logic.

Divergent Thinking (Right Brain)

Could be described as the domain of visualization and intuition. It ena-bles intuition and spontaneous directions to explore and undertake prob-lems.

Convergent Thinking (Left Brain)

In contrast, the left side of the human brain is characterized by thinking in terms of symbols and words. It enables the brain to logically analyze problems and leads to the correct answers.

When both divergent and convergent thinking are exercised simultaneously, it is known as Whole Brain Thinking. The key to groundbreaking ideas is to abandon everything you already know and entertain the impossible. DO NOT rush into action with the first idea you come up with. Below is a list of useful techniques to generate or develop your initial ideas.

- Checklists

- Stimulus materials such as pictures, objects, and words

- Brainstorming

- Mind mapping

- Analogical thinking

- Upside-down thinking

- The Five Ws & H (Who? What? Where? When? Why? & How?)

- Observing consumers

- Seeking inspiration from the unfamiliar (sound from nature, washing machines, etc.)

The Difference Between Creativity and Innovation

*"**Creativity** is thinking up new things.*
***Innovation** is doing new things."*

—*Theodore Levitt*

M any people have used these words interchangeably, but there is an important difference between creativity and innovation. Creativity is the art of having ideas while innovation is putting the ideas into action and changing people's lives. Creativity means having a greater imaginative capability than other people. To imagine is very simple and to imagine great things in life that can be incorporated into music is even simpler. Creativity leads to innovation and for one to act on something, they must have an idea first. It is like the foundation of all businesses and for creativity to be seen, it must be done physically. People who are only creative but not innovative are referred to as dreamers who have the will to imagine but lack the will to act. For an idea to serve its purpose of creation, then it has to be acted upon. Creativity in music is when a musician invents of a great melody or great lyrics that can affect people's lives positively. These lyrics should be able to capture anyone and everyone listening. For people to hear these words, a musician has to think of ways of making the song available to many people at once. Creativity in the music business is the art of writing down ideas that will help a person's talent grow and develop while earning money in the process.

Successful musicians are best creative when they surround themselves with situations that affect people. These situations have to be applicable in the contemporary society. They develop their ideas by watching other people's lives or using their own lives as inspiration for developing creative ideas. They also take risks when expressing themselves and tend to work in an environment that is comfortable and serene for high levels of creativity. When creating a new piece of music, musicians need to have a constant source of inspiration that stimulates imagination and provides keenness for good music. If a group of musicians come together to collaborate, each individual should be included in the decision-making. This enhances the creativity, as each person will contribute through expressing his or her own ideas accordingly.

To really shape your creative capabilities as a musician, one should be continuously taking the time to see where he or she has talent and skills. Exploring one's talent is a good thing because this gives a musician a chance to analyze his or her abilities and points them to the areas they need to improve. Creative efforts for music production also involve revisiting songs, arrangements or compositions that were made earlier. These compositions can be improved upon with the incorporation of fresh ideas from new inspiration. An artist could be just as creative when revising original ideas adding or deducting ideas from his original piece.

Another way of being creative when it comes to making viable music is to travel and observe what other people of different countries go through. If a songwriter or rapper identifies with people of a certain place, religion or culture, they will increase their appeal to a wider audience, which could be of benefit in terms of exposure and record sales.

Innovation is what makes some musicians extremely successful in the music industry. It is the part where a musician who wants to achieve success acts upon the creative ideas they had earlier. Most musicians have the creativity worked out but lack the will to act on the ideas they have. Innovation requires having the passion to put the ideas into physical actions, aiming to affect people's lives positively. As a talented up-and-coming musician, you should learn how to incorporate different materials into your music. These materials should be inexpensive—those of which can be easily found to save time and money. There have been many successful musicians who did not pay expensive producers to produce their songs but produced and recorded their own music using low-priced software and a small room for a studio with just a few pieces of technical equipment.

As an innovative musician, you need to be business oriented giving a value greater than what the listeners expect. Furthermore, when you are in the process of creating your music or music videos, always put the interest of your listeners first. This will make your listeners eager to know you and anxious for the next song. Innovation is taking the simple things in life and applying them in real situations to actually mean something. Musicians should always produce something better than the last so that listeners get something that is of greater value. Remember, everybody is a listener. Your job is to convert those listeners into paying customers who will also shell out for your merchandise and tickets.

How to Create a Research Plan

"Know your shit."

—Cosmo Anderson

A market research plan links the public or customer to the entrepreneur through available information. This kind of information is used to define the problems and identify the opportunities in the market. It is used to refine, evaluate, and generate marketing options for the entrepreneur. A research plan is also used for monitoring the performance of a marketplace and to improve the understanding of any possible business opportunities. As an up-and-coming entertainment entrepreneur, you should create a research plan on the music and entertainment industry. When creating your research plan, before anything you will need to define the objectives for your research project. Below is a set of questions you could use to help define your research objectives:

Defining the Objectives

- What is the core purpose for my research project?
- Why am I doing this?
- What information do I want to gather?
- Why do I need to collect this specific information?
- Will this information help me make better decisions?
- How will it help me make better decisions?

Having defined the core reason for your research project, the next step will be to actually plan the research project. Here you need to decide on the ways in which you would gather the data required efficiently. Research data could be gathered in two forms: primary data and secondary data. Primary data is otherwise known as field research, where the information must be obtained by direct observation. It is useful for a specific purpose and has to be conducted from scratch. Secondary data is where information had already been collected for another purpose. This method is easier to use, as the information is already available.

Your job as a music entrepreneur should be to know and understand the different types of people who listen to your style of music. You should know and understand the different types of commercial places in which music is played (car radio, discotheques, shopping centers, churches, schools, and drama clubs). With this information, you are able to tailor songs and recordings to satisfy these prospects. Prospects could be described as potential customers. Observational research is often used when people are unable or unwilling to provide the necessary information.

Another method is using surveys. Surveys help to uncover the knowledge, attitudes and buying behavior of specific music consumers. This method can also be used to inquire about the customers' preference in terms of songs, instrumentations and recordings. Below is a set of questions you could use to help decide on the most appropriate methods, research approaches and instruments for collecting the information.

Planning the Research

- Do I know how to plan a research project/ if not, should I hire someone else?

- What methods are best suited for collecting the correct information?

- Should I use the primary or secondary techniques?

- How should I analyze the data collected?

- What time period do I have to collect the information?

Primary research methods

- Interviews

- Surveys

- Questionnaires

- Observational

- Experimentation

Secondary research methods

- Online databases

- Libraries

- Books and Journals

- Official Reports

- Government resources

Positioning and Segmenting Your Marketplace

"Sound strategy starts with having the right goal."

—*Michael Porter*

Positioning and segmenting your business in the market place is the most effective tool to aid entrepreneurial decision making. It provides a framework for you to know where your business venture stands in relation to its competitors. Existing competitors leave gaps in the market enabling entrepreneurs such as yourself to fill them. Positioning relates to a location, and location could be described as occupying a space. Segmentation is where entrepreneurs look at the overall marketplace (for example, the urban music market) and split it up into smaller groups, which in this case Hip-Hop is one segment, R&B is another, and soul is a different segment. What's more, you could actually segment even further, e.g. in hip-hop you have additional segments such as gangster rap, freaky sexy rap, club rap, reality rap, or educational rap.

As a musician, you need to know what makes you different from every other musician and how the competition between you and other musicians affects your business. What segment will you dominate? In addition, you will also need to segment the marketplace in terms of gender, geography, age and socioeconomic status. Here, you should know which age group listens to your music the most. If you have a concert, what gender attends your shows the most? Are the people who like your music religious? Are they free spirited people or party people? To have an edge over your competition you will need to know these factors.

This information will enable you position your establishment successfully giving you a competitive edge. It is all about having a competitive edge. Never forget that. A musician should sit down with his research group or marketing group and analyze the segments that are being served well by competitors. Pleasure and social esteem are what a musician should focus on when it applies to individual customers. The musician should be able to satisfy the emotional need of a customer and fan. A musician is advised to produce songs that can change a life or affect someone in a positive way. Ask yourself, why is Stevie Wonder so successful? Why was Tupac Shakur so successful in making people from disengaged backgrounds across the globe proud of themselves regardless of their unfortunate situations? Many people give up on life, lose faith, or believe that there is no future for them. This could be an opportunity for a gifted and talented musician like yourself to take up the responsibility and go deep into your notebook and bring out the best inspiring and motivational lyrics that spell hope in these particular people's lives.

A lot of people all over the world would rather buy music that has hope in it, than music that is full of hate and disappointment. If a certain song makes a person smile or laugh in amusement, then the song has served its purpose of satisfying a customer at an emotional level. Many people buy music that affects their lives in one way or another.

When positioning your music in the marketplace, you need to know your ideal target. Your music is supposed to affect your customers on an emotional level and this will be their driving force to buying your music. The best position of music meant for teenagers and young adults is the Internet. Contemporary society has achieved in distributing Internet services to many places all over the world and teenagers and young adults work and play online. Banking has moved from the physical to the virtual and people hold money in online accounts that they can use to buy music from your music store. Delivery of music is also fast and it takes only a few minutes to send purchased music to the customer.

The highest population in most countries or states is in the urban areas. The best place to position your music is in an urban sector because these segments are the adjudicators. They decide what is hot and what is not. You will need their acceptance. If they like your style and music then the rest will follow. The urban communities make and break artists each and every day. The suburbanites are known to support those musicians who have been approved by the urbanites financially. If you want to produce music that is meant for these urban teenagers and young adults, the best approach is to fully understand their behaviors, attitudes, and preferences towards your type of music and tailor your music around those factors. To achieve success, you have to know what your customers are about. You need to know the economic status of your target group and how well informed they are about your music.

Entrepreneurial Venture and Business Planning

"Shoot for the moon and if you miss you will still be among the stars."

—*Les Brown*

Becoming an entrepreneur is one of the most challenging and rewarding decisions an individual can make. Entrepreneurs praise the flexibility that "being your own boss" offers. However, being your own boss means working long hours, taking full responsibility, and spearheading the entire venture.

In order to become a successful music entrepreneur, one of the first things you will need to do is create a business plan. Business planning is essential for your venture simply because if you fail to plan for your business, you could regret it in the near future. Business plans enable enterprising people to express the identified opportunity and the idea in which to seize that opportunity technically. It will codify all the information you already have about the industry, market, the segmented target market, the competition and the financial requirements to go ahead and make it happen. Below is a simple guide of what type of information you should include in your business plan:

Executive Summary

Here you should summarize the main points of your business plan. The key to an effective executive summary is to only include enough information so that the reader could get a clear understanding of what the entire business plan is about.

1. Business Description

What will your business do? Just imagine that you are describing it to someone with absolutely no idea of your business environment. Here you could describe sources of revenue and outline your business model. Who will you need to involve to make your business work (suppliers / distributors / publishers)? What will you need to do to operate the business?

2. Market Opportunity

What and why is there an opportunity in this market? What are the needs in which your proposition meets? What makes you think that your business proposition is better than those that already exist in the marketplace? Are there any alternative solutions besides your idea?

3. Target Market and Customer Propositions

How many different market segments have your identified? Which ones will you sell to? Describe exactly who they are. What different needs do they have and how will you address those needs profitably? Clearly describe your business proposition for each segment you will sell to.

4. Market Analysis and Competition

Using the facts, describe the market and industry your business will operate in? Are there any changes in this industry and what are these changes? Who are the market leaders? Who are your main competitors?

5. Differentiations and Unique Selling Proposition

Explain what makes you different from the competition. Why will people pay you for what you are offering instead of going to someone else? What is your specialty?

6. Sales and Marketing

How will you communicate with the market? What will you do to ensure that they know you have something they need? How will you promote your offerings to prospects? What is your method of sales (online, retail, etc.)?

7. Management Team

Who will lead the business? What professional skills and experience does the leader already have? Are there any new skills they must learn? Explain the role and responsibilities required to run your business. What key skills are required? How will you source and select these skills?

8. Business Operations

Explain what systems and processes need to be in place in order to successfully run the business—for example, studio, office, bank accounts, and IT systems.

9. Business Partnerships

Do you need to partner with any other organizations (iTunes, Interscope, etc.)? What role will they play? Have you already approached them? Is there a legal agreement in place?

10. Milestones

What have you done so far? What needs to be done before you officially start the business? Include any chronological timetables. Have you made any sales? Do you have any orders?

11. Financial Forecast

Here you will need to include separate detailed cash flow forecasts along with profit & loss statements. It is standard practice to project the revenues for the next three years. How much will you charge for your product or service? How much does it cost you to produce your products or provide your service? What wages or salaries will you have to pay? How much is the rent? How much tax do you need to calculate? You will also need to include notes and assumptions about your financials, e.g., what made you arrive at this forecast? Why have you decided on these values?

12. Funding Requirements

How much will you need to start the business? How much money will you invest yourself? What will you spend the money on? How long will it take to start once you have the money? How do you plan on raising this money? Will you share the profits in return for a cash investment? What percentage are you willing to give? How will you justify this equity share?

Publishing Your Songs

"If it weren't for received ideas, the publishing industry wouldn't have any ideas at all."

—Donald E. Westlake

No matter how brilliant your song may be, it doesn't do you or your audience any good unless it is made available to the music industry and to the buying public. And to do this effectively, you must understand the critical difference between the sound recordings of your songs and the underlying words and music. The underlying words and music is what gets "published." It's how an artist makes money when another artist covers his or her song. For example, when an artist records a song written by Ne-Yo, checks are sent to Ne-Yo. Music publishing can be a huge source of passive revenue. If at all possible, you must NEVER give up or sell ownership of your publishing. Your songs are your products, and you should always strive to retain ownership of them.

Self-publishing facilitates total control over the compositions and its publishing without having to rely on any third party for help with the only limitation existing of promoting your work on your own. This can be achieved with the help of self-publishing websites, wherein potential buyers can download your work for a free trial.

Further, a conventional method to have your work foray into the dynamic music markets is to search for an established publisher who would be interested in your work for which you can scan the Internet for resources and mediums. In order to enhance the scope of work and publishing and improve the prospects of business deals, you can hire your own **personal agent** who will make it easy for you to establish contacts with the industry honchos and even extend a helping hand in marketing and promoting your work, while you concentrate on making new music and honing your musical skills.

Another way can be **recording a demo** of your performance in case you are a singer or even hire someone to sing your compositions. Traditionally, in the modern-day music business and scenario, songwriters do not put up their material for sale, but rather get their songs recorded and released in the market in the form of CDs that are ultimately performed on various radio and TV stations. The publishing procedure depends upon the type of music being made and varies according to this field.

Songwriters and composers can publish their work by being a part of collection societies and registering their copyrighted music works. The self-publishing can be highly rewarding as well with the composer retaining the full royalty after the society's commission is subtracted and therefore does not require splitting the profit with the publishers. A composer can freely approach resources like agencies and music companies that could be interested in using the compositions. Further, external sources like advertising agencies and other media can also prove to be immensely useful in getting the work showcased by using it in films or stage performances.

Music enthusiasts can also contemplate **moving to music industry centers** that are known for publishing agents like Nashville, New York City, Los Angeles, and London. However, you must be prepared for consistent efforts to come into contact with the right organization and since you would be situated in the local area, it would always benefit your credentials. Detecting a small speck of interest from a prospective buyer will help you to get noticed. Being readily available for further discussions will offer an enhanced scope for working out a potential deal.

The majority of earnings made by songwriters come from performances made on the radio and TV stations and since these performances are paid, each time a composition is performed on TV or radio station, a certain amount of revenue is earned by the songwriter; the amount can be bigger if the performance is made on a primetime network. The **performing rights societies** such as BMI, ASCAP, and SESAC along with their affiliates all around the world keep an effectual track of when and where the compositions are broadcast and accordingly play a significant role in helping the composer receive her/her royalty checks for each quarter.

Usually, **record companies and music publishers** are interested in signing up established artists and songwriters who have their own work ready; however some of them may also be willing to sign on fresh talent without a deal, and this can help mark a significant change in the musical career of a new composer. If a music publisher believes in the talent of a composer, and is willing to suitably invest in his attempt, it can produce long-term financial and commercial benefits for both parties. For the present, the composer can record demos and the publisher can assist him in landing new record deals along with having the prospects of public performance royalties and other income derivates.

Strong financial backup is immensely vital for a successful recording career. Nevertheless, any new artist has to shell out his own expenses for starting up the publishing of his work. In case you are out of savings already, lookout for a potential investor in your circle of family and friends who believes in your talent, or even look up to the bank for a short loan. Sometimes, a publishing company may allow you to pay up in the form of easy monthly installments and as the quality of your work improvises and as your talent spreads, eventually you would not have any problem in finding financial backers.

The most efficient resource for locating potential publishers is through the **Writers Market**, which can also prove to be the best source to find a publishing agent or a manager that can contribute towards promotion of your work. There are multiple hard copies available for this purpose that can be found in most bookstores and they also have a dedicated website for same and charge a small fee. All said and done, even if your hard work doesn't pay you at the present, do not be disheartened, some of the major record companies had rejected new talents before they got their big break and became a universal sensation. Therefore, your hard work combined with talent would definitely pay off today or maybe later, hence keep trying.

The most important part of the composer's career is to get their work **copyrighted**. Nowadays, music publishers are increasingly concerned with administering copyrights and licensing the music to the record companies and further collection of royalties on behalf of the composer. To enhance the scope of financial returns, publishers may also strive for effective and authorized translations of the compositions in order to generate income from cover versions in foreign countries.

Overall, the aforementioned procedures and methods can be of great help to up-and-coming musicians in establishing themselves in the aggressive music market and carving a niche of their own amongst the crowd.

CHAPTER THREE

The Digital Revolution

"The digital revolution is far more significant than the invention of writing or even of printing."

—Douglas Engelbart

Overview

Thanks to the emergence of the Internet and myriad of other technical advances we are now experiencing a digital music revolution, which has literally changed the way we enjoy music (iPods, MP3 players, digital radio). In fact, it won't be wrong to state that the music and entertainment world is basking in its best time. In addition, one must also note that much of the credit for making music popular through these devices goes to the Internet from where music lovers can easily download their favorite music instantly. The revolution in the music industry has taken some time to materialize and it has in fact undergone various stages. Earlier people used to play music on 12-inch records (LPs); then came the time of using cassettes, which was then followed by CDs. The ubiquitous CDs in turn were replaced by DVDs and now, with just a pen drive you can carry as many as 500 songs in your pocket. So, from tangible 12-inch records, tapes, and CDs, music has evolved into a less tangible form: digital data. We no longer need to use big and bulky transistors or radios to listen to music, all we need is a PC, an iPod, an MP3 player, or a digital radio to listen to our favorite songs wherever we go.

The Role of the Internet in the Digital Music Revolution

After television and radio, the Internet has occupied the music world with its ease of use to play music. You can get to use the facility of pay-per-view websites for live concerts, artist interviews, retail components, merchandising opportunities, and video graphics. Furthermore, with the coming of new consumer products like HDTV, set-top boxes and home entertainment theaters, the digital music world has got more expansion. Music buyers are happily buying all their favorite music on the Internet. It is all because of the Internet that now we no longer have to rely on radio stations to listen to our favorite songs; we can download them instantly from the Internet. In other words, the Internet enables us to access wider selection of music, be it old or new. Not just for the music listeners, the Internet has become a boom for music makers, who can control their music from the Internet. Music record companies can easily record music and sell millions of copies using the net to save on cost thus making huge profits. You will be astonished to know that even great artists are now choosing to distribute their music through the Internet. On the other hand, some bands are setting up websites to sell music and merchandise directly to their fans at comparatively low costs.

Major Concerns Regarding the Digital Music Revolution

The two major concerns regarding the digital music revolution are time-consuming downloading speeds and copyright piracy. Both these concerns result in a slow pace of growth in online music delivery. The complaint for lengthy download time is mainly due to low bandwidth. Generally, about three minutes are taken for an MP3 downloading over an ISDN line. However, Internet in the sky, a new global satellite system, will enable a user to download MP3 music in just half of this time.

Copyright piracy is the other major concern of the digital music revolution. According to copyright policy, you will be able to easily use, download, copy, and alter music files without any worry. An effective copyright management system will soon make distributing the music files secure over the Internet. Digital radio is also beneficial in its own way. You get to enjoy a better sound quality on digital radio because it is not affected by atmospheric conditions and electrical interferences. In other words, the quality delivered by digital radio is unmatched.

The most popular way of downloading music these days is through iTunes. This online music store enables you to download music on your iPod and MP3 players. You can also organize your downloaded music on your music device through iTunes. iTunes will not allow people to transfer or share music as it aims to support the musicians and labels that own the content to be financially rewarded for their talents and business.

As a result of this prohibition, many music lovers have turned to the use of torrents for downloading and sharing music. However, one must point out that downloading through free torrent services is illegal in the United States. You can download through torrents but at your own risk. An alternative to torrents is downloading music through MySpace. Many musicians and artists directly offer the choices for free downloading of music through MySpace. Ultimately, many people think that the digital music revolution is a return to the 1930s. We can't say that this is true or false, but we can definitely say that the new digital music devices have replaced the old bulky music recorder and gramophones for listening to music.

Digital Music Formats

"Digital for storage and quickness. Analog for fatness and warmth."
—Adrian Belew

Technology has been an initiator of change and every industry today has seen drastic changes over the last decade or two in the very way they function. The music industry too has seen a series of changes and the very way we listen to music has altered. The once mighty gramophone and Walkman have given way to digital music, which has literally changed the way music is recorded and distributed. The digital music revolution has seen the emergence of a host of digital music formats from MP3 to WAV that allow you to save effortlessly whilst enjoying your kind of music. All these digital music formats have changed the music world in their own ways. For example, if one format offers compact storage, another offers high quality sound.

Choosing a digital music format is the most common problem that many people tend to experience today. They are confused thinking which is the best music format for their PC or other portable audio devices. The MP3 is the most widely used digital music format used on the Internet. For a better audio quality, CDs are recommended to store music as they have a higher sampling rate of 44.1 KHz and the audio is uncompressed. Another file format used for downloading music on cell phones is WAV.

WAV Format

WAV or WAVE format is a short form of Waveform Audio File Format. This one is an application of the RIFF bit stream format method that is helpful in storing data in chunks. This format is widely used for storing sound in the form of files developed by Microsoft and IBM. Usually, WAV files end with a.wav extension and are compatible with all Windows applications.

MP3 Format

MP3 or MPEG-1 Audio Layer 3 is a format most widely used for audio files. The Moving Picture Experts Group designed this specific audio format. It is important to know that an MP3 file is created using the setting of 128 Kbit/s. Layer 3 of MP3 files is one of the three coding schemes used for the compression of audio signals. In MP3 files, music shrinks three times as compared to a CD.

We all know that MP3 has changed the music world with its amazing phenomena. The digital music world is now able to listen and collect all the favorite songs instantly with the help of MP3 format. Though some people believe that the MP3 format can't be compared to CDs in sound quality, MP3 formats are popular. In an MP3 format, music breaks down in a number of bytes per second. MP3 format compresses a CD-quality song by a factor of 10 to 14 without affecting the CD-quality sound.

CD Format

Compact Disc (CD) is an optical disc that is used for storing digital data. CDs are developed to record sounds and all kinds of data. This format incorporates a spin-off Laserdisc technology. CDs have the credit of replacing 12-inch vinyl records. A normal CD can store up to 74 minutes of music. This small round piece of plastic is made of injection-molded piece of clear polycarbonate plastic. This disc also has a reflective aluminum layer and a thin acrylic layer. Files are recorded on a CD in a circle movement.

Best Music Formats for Cell Phones

While downloading music or videos on your cell phone, you might have wondered which are the best music formats for your cell phone. The Advanced Audio Coding (AAC) format was developed as an improvement over the MP3 format, and AAC offers better sound quality. Apple uses AAC for its iTunes store.

Best Music Formats for iPods

Usually, iPods support both MP3 and WAV formats. The only format it has difficulty accepting is the WMA music format. iPods have in fact been made in such a way that they are compatible with all the popularly used music formats.

Best Music Formats for iPhone

The iPhone is another widely used entertainment device. The best thing about the iPhone is that almost all kinds of music formats are compatible with it, be it MP4, MP3, AAC, and H.264. You can also download music directly from iTunes on your iPhone.

Selling Your Music Online

"Apple is leading the digital music revolution, but at its core, it's all about the music."

—Steve Jobs

To successfully operate as an independent music artist, one needs to constantly remain focused and make a sustained effort to develop effective networks and contacts. As a musician you would naturally want your music to reach out to all the right audiences and aim at earning decent profits while climbing up the popularity charts. Since the Internet today is the most efficient and cost effective medium available for marketing any business or brand owing to the huge exposure it offers, it is quite logical for aspiring musicians to explore this medium to promote their work.

However it takes much more than just posting one's track online to gain any significant amount of revenue or audience. A musician needs to carefully understand the various factors in play. Music industry websites can be very unpredictable when it comes to helping you to build up a fan base. Further, as digital music is growing in popularity along with accessibility, the sale of physical music CDs is at an all-time low. The best way for you to manage your career and music is to hunt for and cover as many avenues as possible to market and sell your work to potential customers and retailers. While placement of music onto the net is an integral step to promote your music and brand and enhancing the revenue sources, knowing what type of web portals to use for selling your music is the initial step towards making your presence felt.

What Is a Digital Retailer?

With the rising power of the web, music selling has reached new heights wherein online retailers sell music through the web in numerous formats which includes digital downloads on per track or album basis and also through subscription services which provides suitable access to the retailer's catalogue for a monthly fee. Buying music from a digital retailer can prove to be much more convenient and simple for a music buff than approaching a traditional retailer as online retailers have their own promotional programs and special features to promote artists placed in the catalogues. The promotional emphasis is placed on fresh releases and unique content that will garner maximum exposure and publicity. Typically, these retailers request the distributors to submit their music and metadata, which includes information like artist, track names, album, and publisher, along with other vital information in a particular file format that facilitates uploading of information. These digital retailers keep a percentage of each sale and pass the balance to the distributor. Thereafter, the distributor pays the appropriate record label for each sale made that in turn facilitates the payment of the artist as per the terms and conditions of the recording contract.

Digital sales are at an all-time high owing to their simple functionalities and approach along with the cost-effective premise. The cost involved in getting a record to market for digital distribution is much less than traditional retailers since there is no requirement of manufacturing, warehousing, or shipping the music CDs to digital retailers, which automatically reduces the cost. However, besides all the aforementioned pros and money-saving qualities that digital music offers, the main drawback is reduced revenue, as the returns recognized by the distributors, labels, and artists on per-release basis is less than a traditional CD.

Furthermore, digital music can be effectually stored in humungous accounts in computer systems and iPods, which are the preferred option by today's music lovers. There are over 100 million iPod owners and therefore you have a potential 100 million prospects. When selling your music using a digital retailer you will need to let your prospects know the genre, name, and title of the song or album. The relationship between you and your listeners is extremely important. You will need to invest time and money when developing a relationship with your listeners. The fundamental nature of this relationship should be based on respect, trust and loyalty.

Information and instructions for selling music online

Any artist who wishes to sell out his or her music onto the Internet must first and foremost create a website that works as a digital support for all the content you wish to publish. A personalized web page facilitates hosting of varied imagery, text, and music videos along with music that provides maximum flexibility to present your work without any hassle or censorship. This kind of freedom cannot be enjoyed on any third party website that might pose restrictions or limits to publishing your work. Organizations like alarana.net help musicians to create their online portfolios and can be easily contacted if you are facing any difficulty building your own web page.

Furthermore, you can create your very own streaming player that your fans can embed on their web pages and MySpace pages. Websitemusicplayer.com can help you in building this music player and also helps in controlling where and how the music is displayed on the Internet for public access. You can provide various offers to users who place your music player on their websites like incentives or even special copyright freedom. Moreover, the user can also sign up and be a member of independent online music websites like the CDBaby who charge a small amount and facilitate artists to sell digital downloads and even physical CDs through third party partners like iTunes, Rhapsody, LastFM, and many more who provide compensation to artists for selling their digital downloads, merchandise, MP3 tracks and physical CDs through their medium.

Since online selling involves accessing digital tracks, putting up your music in the right format is immensely important for maximum coverage. If you wish to sell your creations in a more conventional manner, then you can print CDs and send them to CDBaby and CD Bathtub for selling. Besides, if you want to move ahead of the CD business and work as per developing digital technology, you can prepare all your compositions in an MP3 format and distribute them online.

Another vital component of selling music online is to getting it copyrighted; and save your music from plagiarism and theft. Get your compositions to the Library of Congress along with BMI, ASCAP, or SESAC and get it recorded in the books as exclusively belonging to you. This form of shielding will provide the necessary protection before your music is sold. Digital selling and accessing must involve the copyright to keep things sorted and systemized along with effectual organization of the listed music.

"Snocap" your music as it will facilitate the selling of any downloads and also license your digital content. This premier digital rights and copyright management system was set up especially for digital music. This facility will enable you to sell downloads through your very own online area while using an affiliate agreement and premade code for your download station.

Most Internet consumers have PayPal accounts, so it would be wise to partner up with PayPal and open a merchant account. This will offer your customers secure protection when making a purchase leaving you with more freedom to do what you do best without worrying about handling personal data and payment transactions. While following all the provided information and instructions to sell your music and create a market for your compositions, care must be taken to keep a track of legal formalities involved and be patient for the end results as there are no shortcuts to success. Any glitch or over anxiety can result in making your efforts futile and unworthy.

What Is a Digital Distributor?

Digital music services such as digital distribution or electronic software distribution is the way of delivering content without using physical media. As the name suggests, digital distribution is about distributing music digitally to the consumer's home and is more pervasive than all the conventional physical distribution media like DVDs. It is important to note that digital distribution is most popular among freestanding products that are downloadable. On the other hand, retail distribution of music is the traditional way of distributing music through retail stores. This method of music distribution was popular until the digital music distribution came to conquer the music world. Remember that to make your work successful, proper distribution is required and nothing is compared to digital distribution. It is the way through which publishers can advertise, fund and even distribute their music product to different retail outlets.

Alternative Distribution Alliance (ADA)

The USA's largest distributor of independent music, both physically and digitally, ADA offers digital services to more than 300 accounts in 60 countries. The company's business activities revolve around marketing and distributing audio and video products on behalf of their clients. To be considered for distribution with ADA, your company should be up and running, with a reasonable catalogue of recordings. If you are in this position, then send an e-mail to distribution@ada-music.com with a short cover letter giving information about your company, including any up-and-coming release schedule and distribution objectives.

For more information, please visit: http://ada-music.com/index.php

Independent Online Distribution Alliance (IODA)

A medium that allows independent companies and individuals to get their work onto hundreds of outlets around the world, IODA offers access to outlets including iTunes, Napster, Amazon.com, Verizon, and many others. The process that IODA uses to get people's work onto these outlets is a unique technology that allows and provides distribution and marketing services for the work. IODA has a special business development team that constantly looks for the best opportunities for ways to get the best deals in order for your music to be heard around the world. Furthermore, this company has years of technical expertise and a great track record to provide your company a competent distribution partner for your work.

IODA has several features that make it attractive to labels and distributors, but perhaps the most attractive feature is that it allows you to create a label store, which acts as a storefront for your music. This means that you can track sales every step of the way. Independent labels can benefit because IODA is specifically made for smaller labels, which means that legal, technical and promotional issues for the label are dealt with. In addition, labels are given 100% control over their musical catalogue, tracking sales and signing other service deals. On the other hand, physical distributors are given an opportunity to get their musical catalogue digitalized and also offer all their labels digital services. In addition, IODA also offers video distribution where your videos can get encoded, delivered to all outlets and what's more, they will collect your royalties for you too. The sort of companies that IODA works with includes YouTube, iTunes, and Amazon VOD.

For more information, please visit:
http://www.iodalliance.com/distributors.php

Song Cast

Once you join SongCast, you can have your music on iTunes, Rhapsody, Amazon MP3, Emusic, Napster, and MediaNet. SongCast will provide you with a special Internet link, which you can include on your MySpace and Facebook pages, so when people hit this link, it will lead them straight to where your songs could be purchased. This feature will make life easier for your fans to find your music online. All you have to do is upload your music, and submit some information, such as album title, album cover, etc., and that's it. Once this is done, SongCast will get your music distributed

For more information: http://www.songcastmusic.com/

TuneCore

Another digital distribution service, TuneCore offers top-notch services to its customers. The main USP of TuneCore is that you own 100% of your product. There are several reasons why you should join TuneCore. Firstly, huge established artists already use the service as their digital distributor; these artists include Jay-Z, Drake, Soulja Boy, Ziggy Marley, and Public Enemy. Secondly, they are trusted by the top digital download websites such as iTunes, Amazon MP3 and eMusic. Thirdly, they have great stats; for instance, in 2009 every second a TuneCore artist sold a song on iTunes. If TuneCore likes your music enough, they will also strive to get you licensing and endorsement deals to be used in TV shows, movies, and video games. They also have an extremely respectable artist support team that helps you with any question that you may have. TuneCore also has an extremely easy accounting system, where you can easily withdraw any money accumulated with a click of a mouse. There are three simple steps to joining TuneCore. Firstly, you need to upload your music. Secondly, you need to upload album art and thirdly, you may select the stores where you would like your music to be sold.

Please visit TuneCore for more information at
http://www.tunecore.com/

CDBaby

CDBaby is primarily an online music store that showcases all the latest independent artists in the world, and they do not discriminate who goes on sale within their store. The company is one of the largest online distributors of independent music available today, and offers a great service to independent artists and record labels. In addition, CDBaby is a well-known music service and attracts thousands of people everyday in search of the latest and hottest talent on show. A few important numbers that CDBaby has achieved are as follows:

278,510 albums sold on CDBaby to date.

$107,769,092 paid directly to the independent artists.

For a one-off fee of $35, CDBaby offers full-album digital distribution. With the selling through the distribution partners option, CDBaby will get your music on iTunes, Amazon MP3, Rhapsody, Napster, eMusic, MOG, Thumbplay, Verizon, and many more. They only take 9% of the net earnings and are always on the lookout for new partners. You can track your sales with detailed reports and not have to worry about the payment transactions.

The second option is to sell directly on CDBaby.com, where customers can directly buy and download your products. Here, independent artists can set their own unique price, with CDBaby paying 75% per download when the sale is made on their site. Even though CDBaby promotes itself as a service to independent artists, your record label can join as an artist. All you have to do is sign up in the artist section and add your label name, and then you can sell all of your individual artists through your account. CDBaby also offers the same service to those who just want to sell singles. With a one-off fee of $9 you could sell a single and have all of the aforementioned benefits.

Please visit CDBaby for more information:
http://members.cdbaby.com/

The Orchard

The Orchard offers full marketing and distribution services that specializes in music and video entertainment. Orchard engages its business activities around the latest business models in effort to deliver the best service possible. The company works with the main digital retail stores, and gives you access to 660 retail outlets in 75 countries worldwide. This is the same with the video aspect of the company.

Please visit: http://www.theorchard.com/ for more information.

Zimbalam

A premier digital media distributor with hundreds of partners around the world, Zimbalam allows artists and independent record labels to sell their music through the most popular digital retail stores as well as mobile music stores. Further, Zimbalam offers all of their artists 100% of the royalty created by the products. Zimbalam is one of the few companies that will pay your royalty and sales monies directly into your account.

There are two ways Zimbalam charges you for their services. Firstly, they charge a one-off fee for distribution for your release. Secondly, they collect an annual fee from your royalties. This fee provides you with storage, royalty reporting, promotional tools, and much more. Regarding the first fee, it depends on what type of product you are releasing. It costs £19.99 to release a single (two track minimum) and £19.98 for an EP or album.

Please visit: http://www.zimbalam.co.uk/index.php for more information.

Ditto Music

Ditto is a digital music distribution company that offers more services for your money than those of its competitors. To expand on the idea of setting up your record label under Ditto Music, the service only costs £25. The label goes under parent group, but you have total creative control over its image and musical output. Ditto Music will do all of the administration work and yet you will receive all of the other benefits of running your own record label. The service provides free barcodes and ISRC codes and will deliver your music to over 500+ digital music stores and distributes royalties of 110% for your music. Their servers are updated every 24 hours so that is very easy for you to know how well your products are selling online. The service also pays you each time you complete a live performance. In addition, your music will also become chart eligible, giving you full control of your content enabling your music to be used in film and TV soundtracks, as they have major contacts with the major film companies. There is a wide range of prices that Ditto Music charge in order for you to distribute your music online. Ditto Music has had unprecedented success in the music industry with seven top-40 UK singles, all with unsigned artists. Ditto is the only independent digital music distributor to have done this. Furthermore, they have worked with the biggest stars of the music world such as Lil Wayne, Prince, and Sean Paul releasing their music digitally.

Please visit: http://www.dittomusic.com/ for more information.

Kudos Records

Kudos Records is a digital music distributor that has the capability to deliver your product around the world. They actually work closely with key programmers at the digital stores to make sure that your marketing efforts result in premium website placement and gain maximum exposure. The unique aspect of Kudos is that they have partnerships with retailers that some other competitors don't have. These include MTV, Virgin, Yahoo! Music, AOL Music, and T-Mobile.

Please Visit: http://www.kudos-digital.co.uk/ for more information.

Marketing Your Music Online

"Focus on the user, build for the long view, and the money will come."

—*Greg Hartne*

Musicians who venture into the music business need to know that when they sign up through a broker, chances are that they will only earn forty percent of the income their music produces. These brokers will take a musician's songs to an online store that allows people to download music from the site then the stores will take about twenty percent while the brokers will take forty percent.

Musicians can market their own music from their own websites. Marketing music over the Internet is not a Herculean task; however it is important to have the right information and procedure knowledge to promote the music successfully. In order to communicate your content to various target audiences, you will need to develop and implement a promotional campaign. There are several main elements of creating an effective promotional campaign, which include advertising, personal selling, public relations (PR), direct marketing, and sales promotion.

Independent music promotion is fast becoming popular, and with a wide variety of options available on the web that can be economically viable, unlike other mediums that involve bigger budgets and campaigns. The main research that an aspiring musician needs to do involves looking for efficient resources on the web or in books, and designing a **personalized web page** to have an online identity. A number of web hosting companies today offer **free website templates** tailored for music artists that you can use after an initial sign-up. Furthermore, many companies can help you in designing your website for a small fee. Having your web page will open the gates of multiple methodologies to reach out to people in the form of newsletters, writing web journals, and even putting up photos or putting up a sale of CDs and music videos along with a forum for music lovers, etc. Sometimes it is helpful to put up some of your music for free on your website that will assist in popularizing your music amongst the desired audiences and will also help in building up your fan base.

Effective **blogging** will also help to nourish networking and connections between you and your audience. Posting regularly and providing all sorts of news and information will certainly nurture such relations. Encouraging your readers to subscribe to your blog via RSS will keep you constantly connected with them and they will have all the necessary updates from your end and direct every fresh post to their mailboxes.

You can also **exchange links** with other like-minded music professionals and mutually benefit from such liaisons involving building traffic to your blog and to others as well. Another method you can adopt to popularize your music is to make it available to podcasters royalty-free who can play it on their podcasts. For them it will be free music, but for you it will be free airtime and space on a medium accessed by multiple music lovers. You can sign up on these mediums and upload tracks to the "Podcast Music Network" and your music will be a part of the official music catalogue and also will be provided with an artist page with all the songs listed on it. So whenever a podcast features your music, you will receive an e-mail with a link to the podcaster's website. These can further garner effective showcasing of your music with minimal effort.

Simultaneously, one needs to set up accounts on social networks like Facebook, MySpace, and Twitter to facilitate building up a brand. In addition, one needs to become active on **social music sites** like iMeem and Bebo that will make your presence felt in cyber space. The social media marketing techniques and viral marketing techniques play a significant role in enhancing the brand awareness and achieving other objectives that are done with the help of self-duplicating viral processes that spread far and wide in numerous virtual forms.

In addition, the user can actively join and participate in **music business forums** and join in general discussions and learn from other participants and also freely contribute to the topic being talked about. Also, you can also provide a link to your posts on the forum with the music uploaded on your personal website. Discussing current music industry topics with professionals and even competitors will only add to your knowledge base and make you more aware of the present economics of the music industry. Moreover, signing up on all major social networks like Facebook and MySpace will assist you in forming groups and fan pages and putting up music samples, which will attract casual visitors and might help you in making a business deal with an industry professional. These networks have a global fan base and membership, and whenever an individual would visit your homepage, he/she can be directed to your music. Using these sites to your advantage will provide a widely distributed promotional campaign, absolutely free of cost.

Concentrate on **playing live shows** and gigs to interact with your audience and to sell merchandise. The immediate connection with someone who really likes your performance will create positive word of mouth and indirect promotion, increasing your popularity as well as brand value. Recording your best live performances on video and putting them up on a video-sharing website like YouTube will generate a stronger online presence and demonstrate your musical qualities and performance abilities.

Invite fellow musicians to visit your shows and performances and **play their music** to your audience and suitably return the favor, hugely benefiting both the parties in capturing newer audiences.

You can also consider in investing a few bucks in having your own **personal radio Internet station** that can further provide scope for a personalized talk show and music broadcasting sessions. Initially you might face difficulty in finding audiences, but gradually your music would speak for itself and you would be flooded with requests and fan mails. Provide **discounts** for your music CDs at the early stages of your musical career; carefully planning this small stuff will go a long way for your brand building and market value.

You can also send your music to be **reviewed online** by industry experts. Start with smaller and minor websites and online magazines that can effectually increase your chances of online publicity, as a majority of these are run and owned by hobbyists and have their own niche audience who are more responsive to these submissions than the bigger websites. A decent amount of space in these mediums can provide the much needed exposure and publicity and can prove to be the link between a mega business deal and your music. Hard work and effective networking is the key to success in this field and as you get your moves right on these lines, you will be able to successfully make your presence felt. Keep looking for newer avenues for Internet and outside promotions and keep building contacts that will generate the much-needed presence for your work. Online promotion requires a lot of effort and efficient networking and any laxity in either of these might not let you fulfill your dream.

One of the cheapest ways to market or sell products and services is through email. Email is proficient and easy to use. Using email to promote your products and services has the advantage of attracting a lot of people at the same time all over the world. It is also important to take the time to write your own emails to fans. This little gesture speaks volumes about the trust and respect that you have for your fans. Despite the fact that emails are a cheap and effective way to reach your targets, frequent emails are frustrating and annoying, especially to the fans. The best practice is to send friendly emails every one or two months. In the emails, treat your customers as if they were personal friends of yours. Emails enable you to update fans on new developments, new singles or albums, new video clips and tours.

Effective Digital Marketing Activities

S.E.O Campaign: (Search Engine Optimization)

This phase of digital marketing will focus on the following activities:

- Organic search engine optimization

- Link building

- Directory submissions

- Article submissions

S.M.M & S.MO Campaign: (Social Media Marketing & Social Media Optimization)

This phase of digital marketing will focus on the following activities:

- Video & article viral marketing

- Social media marketing viral

- Social media optimization

- Flash banner marketing

- Selling advertising space on your website

Email Marketing Campaign

This phase of digital marketing will focus on the following activities:

- Purchase emails of target audience from industry agencies

- Send out targeted emails legally. No spamming!

Web Traffic Conversion

This phase of digital marketing will focus on the following activities:

- Targeted lead generating and web traffic conversion

CHAPTER FOUR

Building a Team

"The Human Brain is like a battery, so the more brains focused on one problem, the more power that will be generated to generate a solution. Teamwork."

—*Isaac Ainooson*

Creating a Vision

"The future belongs to those who see possibilities before they become obvious."

—John Scully

Many big businesses began as small businesses. Every person who starts a business has a dream that sooner or later the business will expand. Having a vision for your business is the best thing you could do for yourself and your customers. Creating a vision as an unsigned and budding music entrepreneur can make you one of the most respected and adored musicians and entrepreneurs.

A vision is what you want your business to be like in the next few years. It is the desire to improve the lives of the people in your community in the future using your music. Most musicians only want to make money and they neglect the need to improve the lives of other people. Having a vision as a budding music entrepreneur is putting the needs of your customers and listeners first before your own. If you want to have a successful music company where you sign recording artists and dancers, you have to create your own vision of what you would like to achieve. Creating this vision will make your life better and also that of your employees. As a budding music entrepreneur, you will need a group of conscious and very knowledgeable people to help you create and achieved a vision for your business. A musician needs to be choosy when asking for advice on the vision for a music business. Very few people know the details involved in producing quality music and selling it to the intended target in the marketplace. Your vision could be how you would like to see the final outcome of your music manifest. Take for example, if you have a vision that one of your beats fit a particular recording artist perfectly, then you have a potential opportunity for that recording artist to fulfill their aims, which is to work with backing tracks that compliment their talent.

A vision is like having hope for a good business when you are still working hard on your current position. To achieve your vision you have to be disciplined and accept your current situation. If you are starting small, then look at it as the foundation of your big business. You have to begin somewhere in order for you to achieve your dreams. This means that you have to consider the most important values in life that help people to achieve greatness. These values are having personal values and standards, passion, working hard, and having faith and self-belief even when the present situation seems hopeless.

People who started their business small did not give up when suddenly their business experienced downturns or failure. They stuck at it pursuing their visions. People who manifest their visions are the people who set their minds to achieve a certain goal in life. Having a vision is like having a dream and not acting on the vision is like building castles in the air. A budding musician can have the greatest vision for his business and it is this vision that will create one of the best and most respected musicians or entertainment companies in the world, e.g. Berry Gordy and Motown Records.

As a musician, you are advised to work on your current music as if it is the next big hit that will lead to greatness. Working as hard as one can is what leads to riches and respect. Having a vision is having the power to positively affect people's lives in the future. Your future starts within the next minute and therefore you ought to act on your vision right now! In fact, by reading this book you are doing just that. A budding music entrepreneur can have a vision of owning the best recording studio in the country or building his or her own music company that owns all the content produced. This can be achieved when the visionary thinks beyond the usual scope.

To bring a vision into existence, one must consider other people who could help bring the vision to life by contributing their own expertise to make up the business. As a talented musician, you need to focus on your own talents and skills, and then employ others who have alternative skills to undertake specific tasks such as marketing, budgeting, and sales. Building the right team is extremely important. Every member of your team should have a skill or an attribute that they can exercise better than anyone else on your team. You will also need a constant source of inspiration as many people have given up on their dreams when they discover that the manifestation of a vision could take some time to be realized. A good source of inspiration can be that of personal trust. Look deep within yourself to bring out your talents, skills and attitudes that could make you an asset to the music industry. It is a known fact that a vision can be achieved when a group of people work together to achieve the same goals and outcomes.

A good and clear company vision enables team members to work with a certain driving force for accomplishment. *Working towards a goal is better than just working*, because when one works and doesn't have a goal or vision, then there is no room for improvement.

A vision could be created by anyone who has the power to think big. Moreover, a vision needs patience and perseverance and for you as a budding entertainment entrepreneur, extra patience is crucial as the music and entertainment industry is an enormous environment with millions of enterprising people seeking success. However, not everyone has the ability to develop an idea into a viable business opportunity through following a systematic process.

But the good thing about the music and entertainment industry is that it doesn't need to be a competition. Musicians and entertainment entrepreneurs can produce music, films, and videos within the exact same category and still have dedicated customers. In fact, there is nobody on this planet who only supports one recording artist or only watches a music video or film by one producer. Millions of singles, albums, music videos, and films are sold each day. It actually comes down to a few factors. Is what you're offering worth the money? Does it make people feel good? Will it provide moral support when in need? If yes, then you should not have any problems selling your work.

Although there are a lot of singers, rappers, producers, record labels, and film and video production companies in the world, many are very rich and successful because they have their loyal supporters who share the same visions as these entities.

What Having a Vision Does

- A good vision will link the present to the future

- A good vision will energize and bring people together

- A good vision will give meaning to your aims

- A good vision will encourage faith and hope

Creating a Mission

"A man with money is no match against a man on a mission. "

—Doyle Brunson

The mission of a company or an entrepreneurial venture outlines the core values and the core purpose of the business enterprise to its owners, its employees, its customers, and the whole community. It is very important because it is what defines the existence of that company or entrepreneurial activity. A business venture without a mission is an accident waiting to happen and until the founding members sit down and define the core purpose of their business venture, the company will be lacking direction.

The importance of creating a mission statement is that people will know the type of services and products you sell. The best practice for a budding entrepreneur when creating a mission is to know exactly what it is you are offering and why. For example, let's say you are an R&B recording artist and you find that your music helps people both in times of sorrow and in times of happiness, you can construct a mission statement that reads something like this:

"I'm in the music business to offer moral support for people world wide."

This type of statement will help you stay focused with a clear directional path. And if you should ever go astray, just take a look at your mission statement and it will put you back on track. A mission statement is also important because it will help you be on familiar terms with your customers and social goals. When you are a budding musician you have to understand that when you put your music out there, people will expect you to be a role model and provide a special type of guidance, one that encourages people to do what they dream of doing.

Almost everybody has heard the song "I Will Survive" performed by Gloria Gaynor. This song is a perfect example of providing empowerment to find personal strength while recovering from a broken heart. The song has such a powerful significance it has become an anthem of female empowerment across the globe. People seek inspiration from musicians with stronger faith then themselves, e.g., the fact that one cannot cure poverty by giving a man food to eat every time he goes hungry. The best way to cure and eradicate poverty is to show man how to produce and cook his own food. The same way with talents and skills, a musician can help people to believe and understand that whatever they put their minds to can come into being as long as they act right.

Sourcing Team Players

"No one can whistle a symphony. It takes a whole orchestra to play it."

—H.E. Luccock

Building a team of players could be a daunting mission. This is because you will need to ensure that you select the right people or work unit for your company. As a talented musician or aspiring entertainment entrepreneur, you will need a group of equally talented people who will contribute and help shape your chances for success. These skills should include a marketer to communicate with the target audience, a business administrator to oversee operations legally, and an accountant to account for the profits acquired from sales. You and your team should all come together to create a positive synergy.

When selecting members for your team there are a several attributes you should look for in order to build the right team for your company.

You must have evidence of the **reliability** of a team member. Your business will benefit from such a team player in many ways. For example, a reliable team player will make sure that appointments and deadlines are met, and things are put in order thus doing their share of the work.

You should always involve people who have the ability to **communicate** constructively. This is extremely important for the success of any business venture. The key is to select people who are not afraid to point out the problems in the company or speak out when they have something to say. Beside honesty, the ability to communicate on different levels, with people from different backgrounds, both written and orally would add more value to your business.

Your team players should have the skill of **proactive listening**. This means that they should be able to understand, incorporate ideas and criticize in an ethical manner. The best team players are those who listen to advice, debate decisions, and come up with conclusions that include everyone in the team. They are active people able to contribute to any discussion.

Passive members are not important to the company because when faced with an issue, they have nothing to say. A problem facing the whole team affects the whole company and it is very important for each member to participate in company meetings. When selecting your team ensure that each person you involve is a **cooperative person** ready to develop trust between the other members. Members of a company who are willing to help each other at any moment putting aside ethnic, racial and gender differences are those who are prime assets to your business. People in a company should know that the contemporary society changes with time and when new things come up, they need to be incorporated in the company.

Your selected members should be **flexible** in their thinking and able to adapt to changes. Changes are bound to happen in any company and the earlier members accept the change the better for the company. Avoid people who are resistant to change as this could prevent your business venture from moving forward.

Quality team players show their undivided **commitment** towards the company and its team members. This type of team player will genuinely try to improve the standards of the company whilst encouraging other members to do the same. Business psychologists have found that when a team player genuinely cares about a company, they will also care for each team player involved too.

Your aim should be to source and select individuals with these qualities. You should take the time to fully understand who they are and what they want out of life. This gesture would be much appreciated by your team players. Remember, team members who are in their correct and appropriate positions are more efficient in the company.

Below is a list of attributes you should look for when sourcing and selecting individuals to work with you on your projects:

- Field expert and fulfillment capability
- Reliable and responsible
- Communicative
- Empathetic
- Astute listener
- Outspoken
- Attentive
- Proactive
- Insightful

Entrepreneurial Leaders

"The key to successful leadership today is influence, not authority."
—*Kenneth Blanchard*

W̶hat is leadership? Leadership could be described as the process by which an individual or a group of individuals are influenced towards attaining a common goal. This process is led by a leader who establishes direction with an effective approach in influencing others to contribute to reaching the desired outcomes. There are several core elements behind the process of leadership:

- It involves more than one person or reciprocal relationships

- It involves working toward a common goal

- It involves creating change

- It needs a key motivator

- It involves influencing others

Successful team leaders know how to inspire, motivate, and guide their followers to phenomenal success. They provide concise, clear, and precise strategic directions, and create ways of preventing subordinate burnout with enthusiasm and also motivation. Your job as an entrepreneurial leader will be to do the same, thus rewarding your workforce for the quality of work or high performance.

Becoming a good leader takes up a lot of time and energy. However, good leaders display integrity, sincerity, and are very candor in their actions. They base their actions on moral principles and reason, never on personal feelings or emotional desires.

As the team leader you should have the ability to envision the future and instill your vision among your team players. You will need to inspire your work force and display great confidence in everything. Those who show endurance physically, mentally, and also spiritually will effectively inspire the employees into contributing everything in their power to also make things happen.

Leadership requires great intelligence and entrepreneurial leaders should study, read and try their best to solve challenging assignments. Business leaders should act with justice; this means that they should treat all their employees fairly. It has been discovered that prejudice is one of the worst enemies of justice. Those leaders who display empathy are sensitive to the values, feelings, interests and also the well being of the employees. The great leaders are those who are broad-minded and often seek out diversity.

Leaders should be courageous, meaning that they should persevere in order for them to accomplish the set goals, regardless of any obstacles. Many leaders display calmness even when under intense stress or pressure. Leaders are those people who often use sound judgment when making good decisions. Hyper-competition in many businesses may force the employees to lose focus on their talent development in the sense that the leaders have to put all their focus and energy on the customers and clients while neglecting the work unit. The employees who are neglected often end up being frustrated and eventually leave the company, and they always take some vital knowledge along with them, leaving behind

empty seats in the workplace that are often costly to fill. To avoid such scenarios, you could apply formal mentoring where individualized feedback is applied.

Leaders need to be optimistic about the future of their company. A good leader is one who has all the hope the team players have lost when faced with hard times. As a leader you will need to tolerate risks or uncertainty. Leaders who accept that they have made a mistake and take the responsibility to change are the best leaders this world could ever have. Some leaders have been known to harass employees because they hold a high position in the company. Whatever your position, respecting your employee should be your first priority because that employee is very useful to the company. Ultimately, you as a leader should fully understand the work force needs someone who they could turn to for guidance. Therefore, you a responsibility to act as the perfect role model for your entire team. Remember, *leaders* are significantly different from *managers*.

Leaders establish direction, bring people together through influence and encourage them to accomplish goals. Leadership is path finding, doing the right things through vision and strategy.

Managers are those who support and build upon the plans of others. Management is path following, doing things right through implementing the plans of others.

CHAPTER FIVE

Setting up Your Own Entrepreneurial Venture

"You need to be ready to fail to be a businessman, not everything you do will work."
—Henry Kravis

Overview

Before you set up any company, you will need to have a legal structure for your business. If you are setting up your company in the US, there are similar options—your business can either be a sole proprietorship, a general partnership, a limited liability corporation (LLC), a joint venture (a general partnership of limited duration) or as a "C" or "S" corporation. If you are starting your company in the UK, you have four options. You can start your business as a sole trader, in the form of a partnership, as a limited company, or as a limited liability partnership.

What legal structure you choose for your business will depend on a number of personal considerations that involve the extent to which you expect to get involved in the company, the extent of your personal liability, tax issues and others. Regardless of where you are planning on setting up your business, you will need to take these important steps:

- Business Planning
- Funding options
- Registering your business name
- Understanding tax and other accounting issues
- Registering for various business permits and licenses

Setting Up Your Own Digital Record Label

If you have a passion for music and keep bemoaning the state of the music industry today, the digital revolution in music has now given you a chance to set up a record label of your own. You can either distribute your own music or those of other independent artists, giving yourself the satisfaction of promoting the kind of music that you like. Though this could be a risky venture, the success of independent record labels such as Percy "Master P" Miller's No Limit Records proves that there is great potential in this field.

Before you start looking at ways in which you can actually set up your own digital record label, you should be clear in your mind about what your priorities are. Obviously, starting a record label in the tough music industry with the intention of simply making a quick return on your financial investment could lead to disappointment. On the other hand, if you are willing to stay committed to the cause, opening the doors of the industry to others who would not otherwise have had a chance and building up a solid reputation, there is every possibility that you will eventually come across bands or records that will bring you fame and fortune.

While you may be in touch with a few artists or bands that you believe have the potential to make it big, you need to have a few additional things formally ready. Most important of these are the title for your record label and some interesting label logo and designs. You should also have identified some good artists and have the music ready for distribution. At this point, it is important to remember that you are not merely considering the development of a website for your record label but also the various digital distribution options that you can make available through it. While earlier there were just one or two options, today consumers have a wide array of gadgets through which they can listen to their music—they can download, side load, podcast, webcast, stream or just share peer-to-peer. Through your website, you can offer fans a one-stop-shop through which they can buy many products you have on offer.

You should however, bear in mind that for the downloads of your artists to be chart-eligible, you have to work with an established partner, one who will provide you with encoding and encryption services as well as the necessary e-commerce facilities. You should join a few official organizations that will help you and your music earn their royalties by collecting license fees and distributing the income to the master copyright holders whenever your music is copied, performed in public or broadcast. While this is not a requirement by law, as you can imagine if you are serious about your business, this is a step that you must take.

Try to understand what information is needed for your record label to become a member of the specific organization, how the license fees are collected and paid to you. Some organizations will also provide you with training on how to handle your music business, publish related news and research and how to contact the government on music-business related issues such as online licensing or the duration of copyright. A list of collection societies is provided in the contacts section of this book.

Rather than go it alone, you could consider using distributors such as Pinnacle that can build entire digital shops for you. You can look at the digital shopping options they provide at www.pinnacle-digital.co.uk. Along with helping you build your own download store and establish an online presence, they can also help you supply the digital content to big retail sites like, ITunes, HMV, Napster, Virgin, Tesco, and Yahoo. As you can imagine, digital distributors can give your record label greater exposure that can lead to higher sales than what you would have achieved had you decided to manage online sales by yourself. You can take a look at companies such as 7Digital that offer a variety of services to record labels. They can build your site for you, manage the schedule of your music releases, and maintain the online store from where the music is downloaded. 7Digital allows record labels to manage their own shop and all sales from the shop are eligible to be ranked on music charts.

You can visit www.7digital.com/audio_download_store.

You could sell the digital music of your label directly to retailers such as Apple's iTunes (www.apple.com/itunes/), which pays per-track or per-album. Alternatively, you may prefer the streaming and downloadable subscription model as followed by eMusic, Napster, Zune/Microsoft and major Indie retailer Rough Trade. As a small record label, you might have difficulty in supplying music in the variety of formats; each one of these retailers seems to demand. For example, iTunes prefers downloads in its AAC format while Napster uses WMA files. Furthermore, you have to manage separate licensing deals and ensure that your music is released at the same time on all retailers.

If you would much rather spend your time and resources on discovering new talent, signing and marketing new artists, then retail relationships might not be for you. Instead, you could save yourself some time and money by going in for digital distributors.

Setting Up Your Own Distribution Company

There is no doubt that music distribution is one of the most important sectors in the ever-growing music industry. While the music and marketing are vital, it is the efficient distribution of the music that forms the very foundation of the music industry. To be successful, even the world's top artists use a combination of effective marketing techniques with a powerful distribution network. Digital distribution of music has opened up new possibilities for not just artists and record labels but for entrepreneurs who have an ear for good music.

However, like with any other company, building and managing a digital distribution company requires diligence, patience and perseverance. Before you start your digital distribution company, you need to carry out a comprehensive research into the kind of music you are going to distribute and what you know or need to know about the target market for that kind of music. You will need to know the size of the market and what your target audience is like. You should get more information about record labels, designers, mechanical copyright protection agencies, contract resources, lawyers and government agencies you need to contact to establish your business. You should start checking out special-interest music publications or online music websites and understand whom you need to speak to for getting your distribution company adequate exposure. Establish some meaningful contacts and get all the relevant information so that you have a clear plan for your digital distribution company.

Take a careful look at what your competition is offering. There are already many well-established digital distribution companies on the Internet today. You have to evaluate how you will be able to project yourself as being different from them.

You have to attract the right kind of artists and bands. For this, you need to have a good ear for music and the ability to understand what could turn into a hit. Offer all your artists transparent deals and make sure that there is a viable market for them. By offering fresh talent to a target audience hungry for that kind of music, you are going to maximize your ability to get the music heard, to distribute the music and make sales.

There are a variety of formats through which you could distribute your music. The simplest way is to create a website for your digital distribution company and accept all the artists and bands who submit their music to your website. You in turn will offer this music to buyers who will purchase and download the music that they like. In this case, your digital distribution company works just like a record store and there is very little promotion of the music as such. If you choose to be a little more discerning, from all the songs or soundtracks submitted to you, you could only select a few to make available for distribution. By providing reviews and other relevant information about the artists you have chosen, you are providing them more promotion.

You could choose to do full-scale marketing for your record label. This would involve trying to convince various storefronts such as iTunes, Yahoo or Virgin to stock the label's music. You have to make sure that you add new releases when necessary, collect the revenues from the retail stores and distribute it to the labels, after taking a previously agreed upon percentage. As with anything that has to be sold in the digital format, the very first requirement would be an online presence. It is better that you spend some time researching various web hosting and web development agencies as it is important for you to choose a host that is reliable, offers you all the features you are looking for in order to start your digital distribution company and can accommodate a growing number of visitors. You might find many hosting agencies that will provide you with just the tools you need to start accepting music and selling them online. You should also consider consulting a lawyer to draw up a digital contract to offer to artists or bands that would like to sign up with you and offer their music for distribution.

You have to be very clear about the kind of services that you are offering, about the kind of promotion you are willing to provide to the artist and his or her music and what you would be charging for these services. While on the subject of contracts, you should remember that you might have to update all the contracts you have signed to accommodate new copyright laws that come into effect in order to deal with various technological changes. The best practice would be to run your contracts through your lawyer every six months or so to ensure that they do not need any updating or to immediately update them if required.

Make sure that your website clearly mentions the terms and conditions under which you will distributing the music of various artists. These should clearly state the criteria under which their music will be accepted, the copyright rules and your privacy policy. As a digital distribution company, you are responsible for ensuring that the royalties of your artists are collected properly and all sales are properly accounted for. If you are serious about your business, you should have a strong sales tracking and accounting system. Remember, for a digital distribution company, trust and reputation mean a lot and you have to ensure that you are accounting to your artists accurately, following the letter of your contract and paying them their dues without any delay.

If you are already in the music field and know a particular style or field of music, it will help you in understanding the needs of the target audience and also how to promote your artists. However, even if you are learning as you go along, it is important to constantly ask yourself why your artists should be choosing you as the distribution company and not license their rights to some other company. Innovative ways of establishing your company will help you attract a lot of good talent. As mentioned in the above point, in order to attract good talent, you have to prove to the artists that you have a well-established distribution network, You can start a newsletter or an online magazine with interesting music industry related news and information that will get the visitors in. You should also publish your articles in other blogs.

Plan an effective marketing strategy to help you achieve the number of tracks that you would like to start your distribution company with. Obviously, the larger the number of tracks, the better you will be able to attract new artists but you should be careful not to set yourself an unrealistic target. Finally, you should consider your distribution options. If you have a good readership for your newsletter or online magazine, you should focus on getting more visitors to purchase the music online. You can then slowly expand to contacting retail online stores to stock your music. Unlike physical distribution of music that has a high overhead, digital distribution can begin on a very small budget and with just two tracks, if necessary. You can build your distribution company at the pace you want, concentrating on music of your interest to begin with, testing other markets as you go along and finally distributing music of other kinds as well.

Setting Up Your Own Publishing Company

The advent and widespread popularity of the Internet and other new media has meant the emergence of new ways and the re-invention of old ways to publish music and also use various compositions. This has made music publishing one of the most profitable areas of the music industry. By simply licensing songs for use in public performances, broadcasting, and over television, a music publishing company can earn handsome profits while at the same time passing on the benefits to various songwriters. You may either want to promote and sell your own music or would like to showcase fresh talent whose songs you have acquired. You can start your own music publishing company and by identifying the right kind of compositions, registering with official organizations, and advertising your services in the right avenues, you can start to make a profit very quickly.

In order to start a music publishing company, there is no doubt that you need to have a passion for music. In order to turn this passion into a profit-making business, you also need to know which songs will attract your target audience and make enough sales. If you are more in the business management part of it, it is important that you hire people who will know how to scout for good talent and where to find them. For example, you might want to go the traditional way: go out to gigs and actually listen to the songs composed, or else you could search through MySpace.

You should also not underestimate how important contacts can be in the music industry. After all, as a new company you are still trying to build your reputation and having your contacts put in a good word will go a long way in making new talent trust you and come to you to have their compositions published.

While there are standard business legalities including licenses and permits to be obtained, as a music publishing company, you should spend some time in working out your publishing agreements. Obviously there will be no single publishing agreement. You may want to have one for a single song, another agreement for future creations, sub-publishing agreements, and so on. It is highly advisable that you have a lawyer draw up the various contracts; make sure that you tell your songwriters or composers to seek independent legal advice. Once you have successfully established your music publishing company, you might want to offer your artists global representation; sub-publishing can make this possible. You should choose your sub-publishers carefully so that your songwriters or composers get maximum coverage, but do not bind yourself to deals that go beyond two to three years. Also remember that you too can earn extra profits by acting as a sub-publisher for music publishing companies of other territories.

It is important for you to understand that an affiliation with performance rights societies is a must if you would like to start your music publishing company. However, unless and until one of the following conditions is true, your application with the society to be recognized as a publisher may not even be considered:

- There is impending release that contains the performance of a song that you own,
- There is impending broadcast of a television program that uses the song,
- The song is to be broadcast on radio.

Ultimately, if any one of the above is true, you are eligible to have your application processed. You should first come up with a creative name for your company; you are required to provide three alternatives. Spend some time running different names by your friends, family and people in the music industry. Pick a name that is instantly catchy and will attract attention. If you are in the US, you are required to clear the name with three important organizations—Broadcast Music Incorporated (BMI), the American Society of Composers, Authors and Publishers (ASCAP), and the Society of European Stage Authors & Composers (SESAC). Since you will be publishing songs of writers and composers who might be affiliated with any of these, it is important for you to clear the name of your company with all three organizations. Each organization has membership fees and you should verify what the membership rules are. If you are in the UK, you should consider membership of the MCPS (Mechanical-Copyright Protection Society) and PRS (Performing Right Society) alliance.

It is vital that you join these performance rights societies as you can avoid having the same name as another music publishing company, which would lead to a lot of confusion when it came to making royalty payments. These societies are fairly thorough about the naming procedure; they make sure that your music publishing company has a unique name and that they do not end up accidentally paying the wrong party. Further, as a music publishing company, there is no point in going to all the effort of printing music, acquiring copyrights, and going to all the trouble of setting up a company when you are unable to collect any performance royalties.

Once your company name has been cleared, you will have to complete the necessary registration procedures so that your business is truly and properly registered. You can now start all your dealings under the new business name such as opening a bank account for your company. If you have any questions or concerns about other legalities that you need to complete, you should contact the local government agency.

Now comes the most important step: copyrighting the songs or compositions that you have in your company. For this, you should fill out a PA form that will register these songs or compositions as published works. Once you have acquired the copyrights of the songs or compositions that are with you, you will have to monitor exactly where you are allowing the song or composition to be used. For example, if the copyrighted song is to be released on records or will be used in a radio program, television program or motion picture, it is important that you fill out both the publisher's clearance form as well as the writer's clearance form from the main organizations.

These forms will help the organizations keep track of when the song or composition is performed on radio, television or in a motion picture. They will then charge the appropriate royalties, determine what percentage goes to the writer and the music publisher, and make arrangements to make the payment. You will be able to find all the information you need to know about when to send out the forms, what forms to fill out and where to send them, in the music publisher's manuals provided by these organizations. It is very important to bear in mind that as a music publishing company, your reputation will lie entirely on the transparency and diligence with which you keep track of the songs you have licensed out. It is important to keep a copy of all the forms that you send to the various societies and also organize yourself so that you keep perfect track of all the songs and compositions in your catalogue. You could consider looking at specialized software such as full-featured music publishing and song-shopping system that will help you manage your music publishing company even better.

Setting Up Your Own Production Company

S etting up a music production company can be highly satisfying work as it helps you to discover new talent and help shape their careers. A music producer has to wear many hats during the production of a music album, taking care not just of the creative parts but also of the business end of things. This means that you will have to supervise all the aspects of the music recording process, from selecting the right artists and the right songs to setting up contracts with session players, choosing the right studio and engineers, booking the production studio, and managing everything within the recording budget. If you are thinking of setting up your own music production company, chances are that you have the necessary musical skills along with an extensive knowledge of various musical genres, performance experience, and experience with sound and music production in a recording studio. All this experience and expertise will be of great help to you when you set up your own music production company.

Today, music production is no longer the exclusive domains of large, corporate labels. Rapidly evolving technologies have brought a simplicity to the set up that makes it possible for even small music labels to produce highly sophisticated music without the services of a big studio.

In fact, some well known music production companies today have their recording studios set up right in their homes. What has not changed is the fact that setting up a music production company even today involves bringing together the best talent and making the best use of resources and technology. If you are considering setting up your own music production company, we assume that you already have enough training experience to take you to the next level. If not, we would suggest that you get some experience under your belt by working with some professionals in the recording industry to understand music production. This will not only give you the experience required to make a successful start to your venture but more importantly, you will also be able to establish contacts within the industry which will help you promote your business.

Once you have the necessary experience and contacts, you can start the process of setting up your own music production company. You will first have to set up your studio with the digital recording equipment that you will need. This generally includes mixing boards, microphones, and speakers. You could either set up your recording station in a rented apartment or simply at home. Make sure that the room that is going to function as your recording station is well insulated. You should take care of the business ends of things by acquiring the right permits and business licenses. You might also want to consult a lawyer with experience in the music industry to set up a few contracts and to understand the copyright issues.

The other important aspects are the name and logo for your company. Bear in mind that your logo will be included on all the marketing materials, both online and offline, and it is important that it immediately catches one's attention. You should establish contact with high-end recording studios so that you could send your musicians to them to record the final versions. You should also draw up a list of equipment and instrument suppliers who will supply good quality equipment to you when you require them. Further, you should also have a list of back-up musicians to use in individual recordings.

In the business end of things, you will have to manage the tax and accounting aspects such as billing, costs and finances. You could hire a professional accountant to take care of these. Similarly, rather than worry about scheduling studio times and taking care of other office tasks, you could hire an efficient administrative assistant. Once you have delegated the business responsibilities, you can focus on the creative aspect of your music production business. You should look at various avenues through which you can get in touch with artists, sound and music engineers as well as record labels whose music your production company can help produce at a professional level. You need to have an understanding of what music might work and how well it will work. You can then offer to record the music for these artists or record labels.

Once you have signed up artists, you can proceed with the actual recording. If you are concerned about your sound engineering experience, you can simply hire a professional sound engineer. This will ensure the highest sound quality for all your recordings.

All that is left to do is create your CDs or MP3s and market the business. There are many ways in which you can spread the word around about your business. As we have mentioned earlier, you should keep in touch with people with whom you have worked previously such as musicians, engineers, record studio owners, label executives, publishers, and anyone else who can help you get in touch with a budding talent. You could also compile a CD with the music that you have produced to give a glimpse of the quality of work that you can achieve. By developing a website, you can give 24-hour access to potential clients who might want to know more about you or get in touch with you. You should not only provide all the basic business and contact details but also give further information that could attract clients such as the services that you offer and audio clips of recordings done with other clients. Make sure that your website appears on your business cards and on all your promotional material. You could also consider arranging small parties or concerts where you could release CDs containing your latest recordings. This is a good way of bringing your clients into the public eye while also getting publicity for your business.

You should consider joining one or more professional organizations. They will help you build relationships and provide practical assistance with legal matters such as contracts and copyrights. You can find message boards, where you could ask for advice from experts, talk with peers or simply pass on details about your business.

Some organizations that can help you with your music production company are:

National Association of Recording Professionals
http://www.narip.com
This organization has a job bank, a database of member resumes and if you choose, you could also opt for any of their educational programs.

Association of Music Producers
http://www.ampnow.com
By becoming a member of this association, you can gain access to essential music production and payment guidelines. You will be provided with sample master recording license agreements as also sample music rights agreements.

Recording Industry Association of America
http://www.riaa.com/
This is a trade association meant for music recording companies and provides vital music industry links as also information about licensing.

Society of Professional Audio Recording Services

http://www.spars.com

This organization mostly provides educational programs and internships for those interested in the music production business. It helps industry professionals to network and contains information about the latest conferences to be held.

Setting Up Your Own Artist Management Company

Artist management companies have an important role to play in the music industry. Their services range from scouting for new talent, promoting their clients, finding work for them, negotiating contracts and fees to overseeing the production work for their music or videos. It is not surprising that very few artist managers in the past have been able to mold the futures of their clients or leave an influence on popular music. However, the likes of Berry Gordy, who managed the entire Motown hit squad, rewrote the entire role of talent management and were ruthlessly devoted to their clients' interests. Along with this kind of dedication to the clients, artist management requires a variety of skills starting with the ability to handle artists with patience and grace, having the passion to help emerging artists with their career, and the practical sense to be able to manage the business end of things as well. The biggest challenge today for any artist management company is to balance the goals of the business that include having a reasonable profit with those of the clients, most whom will demand complete creative freedom. If you believe that you have the ability to juggle various ends of the business and take your artists' careers forward, you should certainly look at setting up your own artist management company.

You can find a variety of artist management companies, from small one-person offices to large production companies, providing a range of talent management services that should serve the needs of any artist. When you first start your artist management company, chances are that there will be very few employees on board and you will be signing up just a few artists to whom you will provide essential management services. Your work may begin with looking for new talent, signing them up, and then working towards increasing their exposure through various promotional efforts. As you can imagine, the going can be difficult at first but through faith in your artists and persistence on your part, you will certainly prove successful in getting your artists good deals. There are some tremendous benefits in starting small. You will form a stable and tight bond with your artists, helping you to focus on what is best for them. Secondly, it is easier to manage the various operational aspects as well ensuring that you are not spending too much time away from promoting your artist.

Once your artist management company is well established and you have the successful careers of a few artists under your belt, you might want to consider expanding the kind of services you offer. Major artist management companies usually handle production of music (music may be produced in-house or other recording studios), sales and promotion, management of various rights issues and of course, general management.

You should also bear in mind that the Internet is making it possible to run personalized marketing campaigns aimed at specific target audiences. Artist management companies will therefore have to address and learn to take advantage of the emerging possibilities for the benefit of their clients.

As with any business, you have to first comply with the legal requirements of setting up a company, acquire all the necessary business licenses and permits, and of course understand the tax and accounting implications. Next, you should consult an attorney to draw up a managerial contract that will specify the services you will be providing your client, what exactly your responsibilities will be and what fees you will be charging. It is very important that the deals you make with your client are transparent and anything that appears fuzzy or unclear to your artist is explained clearly. You should be advising your client to seek an independent legal opinion on the contract before signing up. An artist management company runs largely on the trust that exists between the manager and the artist and it is good to start the relationship without any confusion. The contract should specify what kind of authorization you will have to make deals on behalf of your client, what your responsibilities are when it comes to negotiating the license and other rights associated with the client's work, what fees will you charge upfront and what will your ongoing charges be.

Your contract may cover most of the legal matters that crop up when you are managing your artists career. However, what about the artist's personal life? What role do you play in managing that? In order to handle such gray areas that are not likely to be covered in the contract, you should ask your attorney to draft some specific tasks that you foresee you will have to handle. This will help you handle the artist-manager relationship with greater clarity.

It is also important for you to understand how long you would like the term of the contract to be. Though Colonel Tom Parker might have been Elvis Presley's manager throughout his lifetime, legal experts usually suggest that contracts be of shorter duration, say three to four months, especially at the beginning of the partnership. As you and your artist understand each other better, you can fine-tune the documents to accommodate requests from both ends.

It goes without saying that the part that should be stated clearly and without any room for confusion would be the compensation part. Usually, artist management companies are paid a certain commission of the artist's income. This commission varies from industry to industry; you will need to understand what managers in the music industry usually charge before you start negotiating. You should also draw up a list of expenses that you foresee you will incur when you travel on behalf of your client, and your client should be agreeable to have these expenses reimbursed.

Though it may sound a little pessimistic, it is realistic enough to have a separation clause included in your contract, for both your artist management company as well as your artist. In fact, you could draw up a separation agreement and a general contract. If you and your client find yourselves disagreeing on many aspects of the person's career, it is a good idea to end the relationship without waiting for the contract to expire. Typically, a 30-day notice is all that is required. If on the other hand, you and your artist have had a long, successful relationship, you might want to add other separation parameters such as contract buy-outs.

Finally, you should consider expanding your company only when you have had a few successful clients. Rather than sign up a large bunch and finding yourself stretched, it is important that you sign just a few, focus on getting their careers launched and then consider expanding. Expanding does not merely mean signing more artists. It might also mean hiring help so that you can free up your time and spend it in promoting your business for some time. You might also want to launch more services before hiring new artists. Consider the financial implications of growing your company before you take any major decision. This will work towards the benefit of your artists and your artist management company.

Setting up Your Own Event Management Company

It is possible that for years now, you have been planning successful corporate retreats and sales meetings till one day your boss requests you to organize a small release party for his son's album. With your own love of music and past marketing experience with music companies, you know exactly what is needed and the release party turns out to be a huge success. This marks a turning point and you seriously consider setting up your events management company.

The one key ingredient that is common to all successful events is good planning. However, as you can imagine, not many people or businesses, especially artists or musicians have the time or skills to handle it themselves. Regardless of whether one is organizing a music festival, a large concert performance or a small release party, managing a music event will mean having to take care of a multitude of things such as selecting the venue, seating arrangements, sound systems, and managing the artists themselves on the day of the event. Understandably, people who are able to plan and manage these events are in great demand. If you have good organizational skills, have an eye for details, plenty of imagination, and enjoy the company of people, you should consider setting up an events management company.

Quick Guide to Starting the Company

Before you consider starting your event management company, you should evaluate how much you already know about the business, what skills you possess and how you can acquire more experience in this area. Some of the most essential skills that you need are:

- Good verbal and written communications skills.
- Excellent time management and organizational skills.
- Budget management and financial negotiation skills.
- Experience in marketing and public relations.
- Creativity and imagination in organizing events.

It is extremely helpful if you can obtain professional certification such as that offered by Certified Special Events Professional (CSEP). Clients are generally aware of the amount of study and research that goes into becoming a CSEP and hence are sure that anyone with the certification is a true professional. You should also consider becoming a member of Meeting Professionals International as they offer members plenty of assistance and access to resources.

You might now want to consider what your target market will be. Most event management companies make the mistake of offering to manage a wide variety of events ranging from corporate meetings to music concerts. If you are passionate about music and your strengths are in organizing music events, you should focus on that one area to begin with. There may be a difference in the profitability that different types of events will bring to your company but rather than risk your reputation for profits, you would do better to start off small and then expand your services. Once you have identified your target market, you may feel you are ready to start your company.

But just like with any other business, you should first have a business plan so that you are ready for all the ups and downs of your business. You could contact your local government agency for some resources on how to write an effective business plan. You will also have to provide your business with a legal structure. This may vary a little depending on whether you are setting up your business in the US or UK. Understand what benefits each business structure offers you and what your liabilities will be; this will help you decide what type of business organization will suit your company the best.

There are many other important aspects of the business that you will need to take care of. If you are starting small, you may have to handle all of this yourself, or else you could hire a few staff members to take care of things like accounting and taxes. You might also want to look at acquiring enough business insurance for your company. Since there are many forms of insurance, you might want to speak to an insurance advisor to understand what form of insurance is best for your event management company. Once your company is established, you might want to immediately start taking up a few events to manage. However, without the right infrastructure in place, you might find yourself running around to get things in place till the very last moment. Not only will this not reflect well on your company, it might also have disastrous effects on the event itself. You should therefore get your event management infrastructure in place before you take up any event management. Your infrastructure will ideally include a network of suppliers and some staffing solutions. For example, when you have to manage a music event, you might have to work with a number of suppliers for the music equipment, sound equipment, photographers, florists, etc. Your staffing resources will include administrative support staff, sales and marketing, and also legal and accounting.

You need to have your financial resources ready in order to establish this kind of infrastructure. It is therefore important to know where you are going to turn to for funds. Your company will certainly need access to some ready cash at the very start of the company when you will be setting up your infrastructure, and later you will require an operating budget to pay all the suppliers and staff. You might of course, want to limit the amount of money you need to borrow but remember you will need enough money to cover the expenses involved in managing various events till such a time as you become profitable.

Now that you have set up your company and established a dependable infrastructure, you can go ahead with your event planning services. As we have mentioned earlier, it is important for your company to focus on some core services at the beginning. Even when it comes to managing a music event, you might want to handle just one particular aspect of the planning such as selecting the venue and getting it ready. As you gain more experience and establish more contacts, you could go into catering, gifts, transportation, communication services for the event and the artists; in other words, full service event management.

As you are deciding on the kind of service you are offering, you should also give consideration to the kind of fee you will be charging. You will have to charge enough so as to cover your expenses and help your company make a decent profit. There are different fee structures that you could consider including a flat fee, percentage of the expenses involved, an hourly rate, a combination of the previous two, or a commission rate.

The final step is to market your business through the right avenues. While you need to have a comprehensive marketing plan, it is very important to understand the influence a good company website can have on your prospective clients. You could provide all the details of your business, list events already managed, provide testimonials of satisfied customers, and show some clips of music events that have been managed by your company on your website. Include your website in all your promotional and business material such as business cards, client agreements, and proposals.

Setting Up Your Own Music Marketing Company

The music industry today is very different from what it was five to ten years ago. Not only has the business model changed but ways of recording music, distributing music, and marketing music have seen many changes. There are now many more options for an artist, musician, label, or music producer to market their music. A music marketing company makes it possible for these artists to take full advantage of both the traditional and new ways of marketing music by providing them with a comprehensive marketing plan.

A music marketing company today will handle the five key areas of music marketing:

1. **Radio and television.** Marketing on the radio or television is probably the most expensive part of any marketing budget, and for an artist who is just starting out might be too much to aim for at the very beginning. Once the artist is well established, it might make more sense to plan for radio or television exposure.

2. **Public relations** involve spreading the word around about the artist or band. While your company can start by focusing on local music magazines, you might eventually want even the big

media magazines to take notice of your clients. You will therefore have to come up with strategies that will help set your artists apart from the crowd and be noticed.

3. **Live performances.** Naturally, gigs are a great way of getting the sound out; your company will need to find suitable venues and time the gigs carefully so that the artists are not overly exposed. These are also great opportunities to sell merchandise, hand out sample CDs, and make reviewers take notice.

4. **Retail music.** You can market your clients to retail stores, both offline and online. Once there is a buzz about and a few good reviews in music publications, you have a better chance of making sales to these retail stores.

5. **Online music marketing** is an integral part of any music marketing plan and this does not just involve developing a website. You can easily upload a few audio clips of your artists' upcoming releases or even make a few tracks available for free downloading. This will ignite the curiosity of your visitors and also help build a relationship with fans of your clients. You could use social networking sites such as MySpace or Facebook to inform everybody about your artists' and bands' upcoming gigs and live shows, post blogs, and make music available for downloading after purchasing.

Opening a music marketing business involves completing all the legal formalities as you would for any other business. Any prospective business owner will have to:

- Decide on the legal structure for the business
- Register your company and obtain the necessary permits and licenses

- Consider renting an executive office to conduct your work from

Even if your music marketing company is a one-person show to begin with, it does not look professional or businesslike to have a home-based office. Instead you should consider renting an executive office in an office building so that you can hold formal meetings with clients there.

Once you have established your music marketing company, you might want to decide what the focus of your company is going to be. Are you planning on working with just individual artists who work in a particular genre of music or would you rather market bands? For example, you might specialize in marketing the music of new country singing talent. For this, you might want to research the market a little and understand where your competitive advantage might lie. You will also need to be constantly on the lookout for new artists and new talents. You might want to host a regular open mike night at a suitable venue where new artists are given a chance to showcase their talents. The most important task that you as a music marketing company will have to do for your client is to create an effective marketing strategy that will cover radio, print, nightclubs, mixed promotions, online marketing and many more. You might even consider preparing press kits and taking care of the client's image. However, for all this to happen, you will need a solid marketing plan in place.

Always remember that a marketing plan will continually change as you try to achieve the goals that you had set for yourself and for your client. A marketing plan that worked well for one artist might not work for a band. You will have to consider the strengths and weaknesses of each client and customize the marketing plan according what you think will work best for them. Also, you need to consider what the market conditions are at the time. Some things that should be clearly stated in a market plan are the goals that are to be achieved. What are you trying to gain for your client? A record deal? Your own digital sales? Are you trying to increase the exposure of your client across the country? State in measurable terms exactly what you aim to achieve by the end of a certain time frame. Make sure that your goals are actually achievable.

As we had mentioned, it might not be possible for your clients to be immediately featured in major music publications especially if he or she is a new artist. Stick to contacting local publications and online magazines. Once you have identified a set of achievable goals for your client, you might want to include the following points in your marketing plan.

- Clearly define the niche audience that you are going to target. For example, you might want to focus on R & B fans in their 30s-50s or college kids who are into rock and roll. Decide whom you want to reach out to and what are the media through which you can reach them.

- If you were planning on some exposure in the press, what would be best for your client national, regional, or college magazines? Would you need the services of an independent publicist?

- Radio and television are excellent marketing mediums, though a little expensive. You will need to identify the stations or the channels that are popular in your target market. You might also want to consider getting in touch with independent radio or television promoters.

- You should consider contacting retail stores in your target market, a large section of who might already be buying online. Target chain stores and special market programs.

- Understand which social networking sites will give you maximum visibility. Keep your site and your profile on these sites updated with news about new releases, upcoming shows and interviews.

- Last but not the least you will need to know what kind of promotional material and merchandising will help increase the sales of your clients. Advance CDs, posters, T-shirts, cups, and key chains are always popular. The more creative you get, more the publicity your clients will get.

Setting Up Your Own Music & Media Company

Often media consultants are referred to as public relations consult-ants or marketing consultants or even advertising account execu-tives. In reality, a media consultant is all this and much more. As a music and media consultant, you have the responsibility of creating strategic plans that will help your clients who may be performers, songwriters, or composers gain a positive and widespread exposure in the press. Many artists, musicians and record labels are not very sure how to make their presence felt in the press as they have neither the skills nor the experi-ence to come up with creative advertising campaigns. Therefore most of these artists, record labels or even talent managers hire outside help to assist in the creation of effective advertising campaigns. Since music and media consultants have the experience in knowing what ads would be effective in which media outlets, they can create cost-effective ad cam-paigns. After speaking to the clients and understanding what the target market is, media consultancies can place ads in only those media outlets that have the best chances of providing a good return on the investment made in the campaign.

Before you set up your own music and media consultancy, you should understand the range of services that these consultancies typically offer and what you would like to start with. For example, some media con-sultants will only offer to place advertisements in various media outlets to gain maximum coverage. Others might offer the full gamut of marketing and advertising services. If your music and media consultancy is only offering very basic media consultancy services, then your job might be limited to simply placing advertisements in different advertising venues. You will be provided with an advertisement copy and will not be involved in the creation of the copy.

You may want to go a little further and offer limited copywriting and production services along with placement of advertisements and buying. If you decide to set up a music and media consultancy that offers more than just the basic services, then your company might have to look at writing copy for radio commercials, working on effective advertising slogans, creating television commercials, and also working on print advertisements. For this, over the years, you will need to build a network of contacts within the media industry. On behalf of the clients you represent, you can buy space or time in the media, placing ads strategically so that they gain maximum exposure and provide good returns on your investment. As a music and media consultant, you will be a valuable resource to any business, as your expertise with various media outlets will allow you to decide what combination of marketing, advertising and public relations campaign will work best for your client.

A marketing consultant probably offers the most varied but comprehensive services. Starting with identifying the target market for your clients, the consultancy will try and understand the kind of brand that the client wants to build and will create a core message to reflect that image. Of course, the consultancy will also come up with a comprehensive marketing plan for the client. It is important for your company to realize that choosing a music and media consultant can be a difficult decision to make for your client. After all, they want to make sure that their money is being well spent and that they can hope to achieve significant returns on their investment once the campaign is over. Many clients believe they can handle ad placement themselves but end up running them in venues that are least visited by the target audience, ending in a real waste of money. Or they may decide to run cheaper advertisements that can again end up backfiring as potential customers might be put off by the non-professional look of the advertisement.

Once you set up your music and media consultancy, you should be able to explain clearly and with figures, why you believe that by placing well-designed advertisements in more expensive spots, your client stands to gain more, as by the end of the campaign they would have reached a much larger and wider audience. Provide potential clients with a list of references whom they can contact in order to understand how you can help them. Finally, you should offer your clients your most basic services such as placement of ads and buying; if they are satisfied and have more funds to spare, you could offer them copywriting, production, and other services.

You have seen the rapid way the Web is transforming itself into a huge network where friends and family can easily interact with each other and exchange news and views. As more and more people are interacting online through social networking sites such as Facebook and MySpace, your clients too have taken notice of this growing trend. They might have even heard of the way many major businesses are incorporating online media marketing as an integral part of their overall marketing campaign. Obviously, as a media consultancy, you have to offer your clients the best in social media marketing.

If your clients are still not very sure of the way social media works, you have to make them aware of the impact it has had on the way the customers, who buy their music, talk about and share their experiences. For example, a customer who has bought a record of one of your clients and is highly impressed by it immediately logs on to her Facebook page where she writes in her thoughts. These are instantly conveyed not just to her friends and family but also to thousands of others who are in her friend network. This and live feedback of this kind will no doubt influence the purchasing decisions of many of those who are in the network. Social media has changed the way businesses operate since opinions can no longer be controlled by positive press coverage or slickly produced advertisements. By including social media marketing in your services, you will be helping your client navigate the brave new world of social media. You will help your clients understand that social media sites can offer them the best visibility and increase their potential benefit. There are many sites on the Internet and as an expert, you have to decide where to invest the time and build the profile. Of course, unlike advertising or marketing campaigns that would end at some point in time, online media campaigns are more or less an ongoing process. Profiles built on Facebook, Twitter, or MySpace have to be regularly updated to indicate new release dates, upcoming shows and gigs, and also provide audio clips and perhaps make some songs available for free downloading. A very wide audience knows every interaction that your client has with online visitors and it is important that you have a strategy planned for each interaction that your client has on these social media sites. By managing their offline profile and online interactions carefully, your media consultancy can ensure that you can establish and build a very enviable reputation for your clients and their talents.

Setting Up Your Own Video Production Company

Recent technological advancements have meant that the size of video equipment has gone down while their sophistication and the quality of videos that can be taken has gone up. Further, it now costs much less to own a reasonable set of video producing equipment. This makes setting up a video production company one of the more profitable ventures in the entertainment industry. Many enthusiastic entrepreneurs recognized the potential in this industry and have invested in video production at a fraction of the cost that the big production companies would have borne. This has, however, in no way affected the quality of the films or the creativity of the artist. If you enjoy video recording and spend hours editing to get just the right look and feel, perhaps a video production company is the right choice for you. It is true that you could start your video production company with just some basic equipment and a few high-end video-editing applications in your computer. But if you are serious about your business, you should invest in proper infrastructure so that you can earn healthy profits and grow your business.

If you have decided to start your own video production company, you will need to identify who your immediate target customers are going to be. If all the experience you have had is in amateur filmmaking, you should probably target amateur moviemakers.

On the other hand, if you have spent a few years in a major video production company and have managed to learn the ropes of the business, you might aim at the professionals in the industry. Identifying your target market will help you narrow down the type of services you can offer them which in turn will give you an idea of the kind of infrastructure and financing you will need.

Once you know the kind of clients your video production company will be getting, you will have to make the tougher decisions about what facilities you will need as also what hardware and software you will need to purchase. Though you might not want to buy very fancy equipment, you have to be prepared with a substantial down payment for quality equipment. Only high quality hardware and software will give you videos of high quality and drive clients to your video production company. You might not require the most expensive equipment or software; research the possibilities so that you can get the best equipment in the budget you have allocated.

Obviously, having to purchase all this equipment and having to purchase or lease some space for video production is going to cost you money. Before you start your company, draw up financial plans on how much money you will need before your company starts making profits. Some of the money can come from your own investments, you could borrow some from family and friends, and the rest could be covered through a combination of grants and loans. Another good idea is to make a priority list for all the equipment required and buy only the very essentials right away. As you receive more funds or your company starts to make profits, you can invest in equipment of lesser priority. You could either rent out space for your video production studio or start one in your home. You have to ensure though that the room is easily accessible and properly soundproofed.

Before starting on any assignment, you should have checked all the equipment to make sure that it is in proper working condition. If you have the right kind of editing software, you could also complete all the post-production editing work in your studio on the computer. In addition to the actual video production and editing part, you will also have to take care of some business aspects of your company. You should have enough accounting knowledge to accurately keep track of all the expenses, of the income derived from various assignments, and know what tax liabilities you have and how to deal with them.

You should also look at getting not just general business insurance for your company but special coverage for all the expensive equipment that you have invested in. Further, you should look at obtaining some storage space for all the video equipment that will be needed on-site as also a vehicle for attending to field assignments.

Now that you have set up your video production company and also taken up a few assignments, your next step should be to promote your video production business so that you can attract more clients. If you are aiming more at the local market, you could contact local businesses, such as ad agencies, printers, local schools and colleges, bridal shops and broadcast stations. You could speak to media representatives of local newspapers to feature your company in their publications. Offer discounts to the first few clients and have some starter specials. Make sure that you have a few video samples ready on DVD to show to potential clients. A business website that contains all the details of your company along with video clips of some assignments that you have completed with testimonials from the customers will go a long way in establishing trust.

If your video production company successfully provides the basic services that you had planned for, you might then consider expanding the business. As a first step, you could consider simpler services such as providing still shots from the videos, copying the video to DVD, transferring to tape, and duplication services.

By picking up skills such as digital video editing and video effects and also learning to handle more sophisticated video production software and photo software, you can offer for sale a variety of products such as clip montages, video slide shows, and many more. Another idea is to offer digitizing services wherein you can convert old videotapes into digital video formats and make them available on DVDs. Also, traditional media is now losing its hold and online digital media is what is attracting even major companies. More and more users are spending their time on the Internet and statistics reveal that there is a sharp movement away from television and other traditional media towards the Web for video and other rich content. In other words, more and more companies are going to want to create digital videos for the web. You can gain an entry into this ever-expanding market by offering digital video services and also consulting online.

Many small and big businesses are using corporate videos to highlight products or services that they are offering. They could also use them for training purposes or to promote the company. These videos could be featured on the company's website, or relayed on screens in the company offices. While not requiring the same kind of resources as television commercials, they are still very effective in promoting more visibility to the company and enhancing their image.

As you can see, a video production company can be started with as little a budget and in as limited facilities as you can afford.

CHAPTER SIX

Legal Contracts and Content Ownership

*"And I would argue the second greatest force
in the universe is ownership."*

— Chris Chocola

Overview

Coming up with a great idea for an invention or a new business is an exciting time. Along with the thrill of a new project is the very real chance that with a lot of hard work, and a little luck, your idea will be the next big thing and you will reap the huge financial rewards. To ensure that your pot of gold is waiting for you at the end of the rainbow, there are a few things that you should make sure to take care of at the onset of your business venture. Among these are considerations for trademarks, intellectual property, and patents. As daunting as the process might sound, it doesn't need to be and the benefits almost always outweigh the costs. Below is some information and links to help you protect the idea that you have developed.

Copyright Protection

Copyright protection relates to creative work in the field of literature, music, drama, choreography and visual arts, among others. The copyright law gives creators ownership rights to economically benefit from their creation as an incentive or encouragement for further creativity. For instance, a lyricist has the right to charge money from a studio to broadcast or televise his song.

Trademarks

A trademark is a symbol that represents that the name, logo, word or symbol attached is coming from a unique source. Trademarks do not have to be registered by law, but it is a good idea since they may not be enforceable outside of a very limited geographical area if unregistered. In addition, registration may be required to globally record your intellectual property.

Intellectual Property

Intellectual Property is a class of rights that protects the ownership of exclusive rights over material created by the mind. Some examples of works covered by intellectual laws are: books, movies, music, paintings, photographs, and software.

Patents

Patents protect inventors from having their ideas copied or exploited for a fixed period of time. Acquiring a patent begins with finding an attorney who will conduct an elementary records search to ascertain whether or not your idea is eligible for a patent. There are costs involved and the laws vary from region to region, but if you have what you believe to be a great idea for a new product, process or solution, a patent is a must.

What Does Copyright Protection for Musicians Entail?

When a musician has ownership rights over his song, it means he can control its usage. Artists having copyright protection over their music enjoy some exclusive rights including:

- The right to reproduce the copyrighted work, the duplication can include making printed or digital copies, recordings, CDs, videos or motion pictures.

- Create adaptations, derivative works or even make revisions and other arrangements.

- To publish, distribute, or sell prints and digital recordings of the work.

- Synchronize the work of art with visual imagery, be it video or film.

- Perform or present the work in a public space.

- License or assign your copyright to another person who then possesses the right to do the above.

How to Protect One's Music Composition

Any work of art produced automatically comes under copyright protection. However, in case of a breach of law, you can follow two simple steps to deter infringement of one's music composition:

1. Marking the work. 'Marking" means writing a properly worded notice. Such a notice, in addition to stating that the law protects the artwork, would prove the creator's knowledge of copyright laws, thus preventing any unlawful attempts.

2. Register the composition. In case of any dispute regarding your copyright, you need to provide evidence. Therefore, it is crucial to register a work with a reputed copyright registration service, which will offer verifiable testimony to the date and work content.

Some Conditions Applicable to Copyright Protection for Musicians

The ownership rights over a piece of music will be applicable only when certain conditions are fulfilled (as specified by the copyright law):

- The creative work must be displayed on a concrete medium. In case of music, the notation must be put down in black and white or recorded on a CD.

- The music composition has to be original, which means that it must be entirely created by the author or at least add minimal amounts of creativity.

Copyright protection will last for a fixed time duration, that is, the musician's lifetime +70 years. The Constitution authorizes this limitation of duration on grounds that old and forgotten songs can be refurbished and given a new life for a new generation of listeners.

Non-Disclosure Agreements

A non-disclosure agreement or NDA is a confidentiality agreement, an inexpensive way of protecting one's business idea(s). It is a legal agreement between the creator(s) of an artwork and another party. In such a contract, the artist discloses information related to the work of art to the second party and in return elicits a promise to not reveal the information to anyone else. An NDA allows the creator of an intellectual property to share his ideas with a partner, distributor or adviser, while legally forbidding the other person from passing on the information to a third party or competitors. Non-disclosure agreements are tailor-made to suit the requirements of the secret holder.

Non-Disclosure Agreements can cover:

- Intellectual property, such as a piece of music, literary work, drama or choreography

- Commercial information, trade secrets, a formula, program, process, drawings designs

- Business plans

- Employer-employee relationship

- Customer and prospect lists

Preparing Non-Disclosure Agreements

Non-disclosure agreement templates can be purchased off the shelf and then adjusted according to one's needs. This low-cost procedure allows the reuse of templates. One can purchase the agreement from the Compact Law site. Download the PDF file (391K) of the contract form from the Intellectual Property Office site. In case a non-disclosure agreement is flawed, which can occur when the definitions are not specific, the agreement will not offer the requisite protection. One can ask a lawyer to draft the confidentiality agreement for maximum protection.

Non-Competing Agreements

For those who are starting a music company, it is absolutely imperative to use non-competing agreements to forestall loss of valuable business secrets and prevent poaching of employees. A non-competing agreement is one in which an employee agrees not to continue in the same profession or become a competitor of the former employer after termination or resignation. This kind of contract is premised on the likelihood that after quitting a job, the employee might start working for a competitor or establish a similar business. In the process, he or she might abuse the ex-employer's confidential information to gain a competitive advantage.

By signing such a contract, the employee promises not to engage with a direct competitor for a specific time period after leaving the company.

When is a Non-Competing Agreement Enforceable?

In this volatile job market, Non-Competing Agreements are extremely effective in protecting one's business. However, it is important to remember that the legal system places great value on an individual's right to earn. Therefore, the agreement must include enforceable clauses so that it does not end up being interrogated by law enforcers. For this purpose, it is important to:

1. Have a sound business reason. An employer must have a good reason for wanting an employee to sign the contract. It must necessarily not be an attempt to ruin a person's career or a punishment for quitting the job. To increase chances of success, an employer must use his discretion and ask only selective employees to get into the contract. The law will enforce this agreement on employees only if the person possesses important trade secrets.

2. Provide a benefit to the employee. It is also obligatory for an employer to provide some benefit to the employee in return for the promise. Offering a job, which is second to none, is one of the best ways of providing a benefit.

Licensing Agreements

Licensor: The licensor is the copyright owner who grants permission to the licensee.

Licensee: The licensee is the company that whishes to exploit the copyright for profits.

Licensing is a contractual right, a permission given by the copyright owner (licensor) to the (licensee) to exploit the musical works in accordance with the license agreement. A good example of a license agreement is where an artist who has his own music production company agrees to authorize a record company to manufacture, market and distribute their musical works. Many independent labels have made millions thus retaining the rights to their content as well as kept their overheads down to a minimum using this model for business. The advantages of this business model for independent artist besides keeping the rights to their works is that they can permit licenses to different companies in different regions for maximum exposure. For example, the licensor could license to one company in the US, another in Europe and one in Asia. All of these licensees will exploit the same content using the same processes but in exclusive regions.

A copyright license can be either exclusive or non-exclusive.

Exclusive Agreements

An exclusive license is where the copyright owner authorizes the rights of their content to only one legal entity (licensee), e.g. a music publisher or a record company. The law states that this must be done in writing, signed by or on behalf of the copyright owner, authorizing the licensee, the exclusivity where everybody else including the licensor must adhere to the rights granted. In other words, the moment the copyright owner has granted permission to the rights of that content under certain terms and conditions, e.g. the terms and condition may refer to a geographical area, a method of production, or production of a specific product. It is illegal for those exact rights to be granted to any other party.

Non-Exclusive Agreements

A non-exclusive license is where the copyright owner will grant the exact same rights to as many licensees as possible. This particular license does not have to be in writing although it usually would be. With this agreement the licensee does not have the right to take legal proceedings if they discover that another party is also exploiting the content. However, the non-exclusive license requires that the copyright owner must take legal action against any infringement.

Territory

When the copyright owner agrees to authorize a third party to exploit their content, the agreement must contain a clause that sets out which territory(ies) the licensee must pertain to. For example, say you are the copyright owner of the musical works a Japanese advertising agency wishes to use in a TV advertisement. You will issue the agency a license with a territory limited to Japan only. Invariably, the license will need to contain the word "World" if you decide to permit the licensee the right to exploit the musical works globally.

Term

Usually, a license is only valid for a set period of time. Therefore, the term is the length of time until the agreement between the licensee and the licensor expires. There are many reasons why period terms are important, for example, it will protect the copyright owner if the market conditions change and the value of the license increases. The standard term compromise between the licensor and licensee is approximately five years.

Mechanical License

A mechanical license is the written permission, signed by or on behalf of the copyright owner authorizing companies the right to reproduce a specific copyright in "mechanical" form, e.g. the right to manufacture and distribute the musical works for use on records, tapes and CD/DVD.

Digital License

A digital license is the written permission, signed by or on behalf of the copyright owner, authorizing companies the right to reproduce a specific copyright in digital form, e.g. the right to reproduce and distribute full downloads, limited use downloads, and on-demand streaming.

Music Contracts

The entertainment industry no longer remains the prerogative of the elite or influential class. With a large number of aspirants entering the circuit each year and the cutthroat competition in the music industry, everyone needs the security of contracts. Contracts are a crucial part of most relationships within the industry. For musicians, it is absolutely crucial to have an understanding or some kind of music contract to protect your works of art. While some are comprehensive and specific to the number of services offered, others are all encompassing. Therefore, having a basic idea about the kind of music contracts one can choose from will prove useful to an aspiring music professional. There are several types of contracts in the music industry some of which include:

Artist Recording Contract

This is a direct contract between an artist and a studio for specific recording purposes. The provisions would outline the compensation for the artist and others who perform on the sets.

Artist-Record Company Contract

This is an agreement between an artist and the recording company, wherein the artist hands over the rights to handle the marketing and allocation of recorded materials to the company.

Assignment of Copyright

This agreement assigns the rights to market to a particular individual or company, on behalf of the artist. The contract is a form of guarantee to the entity that devotes time on formulating marketing strategies. However, it is not a transfer of ownership. The lyricist or musician continues to retain the copyright.

Collaboration Agreement

This contract is imperative in a collaborative job. It details the degree of ownership between two or more persons. This is particularly vital in a long-distance partnership, where artists know each other only via telephone calls and online correspondence.

Co-publishing Contract

This usually takes place between a smaller entity (individual or company) with an established publishing house. Such an agreement facilitates the smaller publishing house to accumulate a fraction of the profits for acting on the artist's behalf.

Publishing Contracts

Music publishing refers to promoting a musical composition and crediting the work to an appropriate artist, rather than actually printing or recording it. Publishing being one of the most lucrative fields in the music industry, artists and lyricists should safeguard their publishing rights. There are seven basic types of music publishing agreements:

A. Single Song Agreement. This is a deal between the lyricist and the publisher, wherein, the former allows certain rights to the latter with regard to one or more songs. This contract facilitates the writer to get a one-time advance that can be reimbursed.

B. Exclusive Song Writer Agreement. This contract allows a lyricist's services to be bought by a publisher for a specific time period. During this time, the writer offers exclusive services and grants all profits to the particular publisher. Such dealings are made only with established lyricists.

C. Co-publishing Agreement. This is the most common dealing between a writer and a publisher, through which both become co-owners of the copyrighted musical compositions. Usually the royalties are split 50/50 (although not always).

D. Administration Agreement. This takes place between a lyricist or a publisher and an independent administrator or a larger publisher. The writer self-publishes but licenses the songs to the publisher for a specific time period and agrees to split the royalty.

E. Collection Agreement. In this deal, the writer retains ownership of the work but grants the rights to collect and distribute the royalty income to the publisher.

F. Sub-publishing Agreement. This kind of a deal is made between a home and foreign publisher. The home publisher, while retaining the copyrights, allows the foreign counterpart (sub-publisher) to collect royalties from certain foreign territories on the home publisher's behalf. The sub-publisher's zone of activity is generally limited to some territories, including the EU, Latin America, Austria and Switzerland.

G. Purchase Agreement. This is signed during the (complete or partial) merger of two publishing companies.

Associations and Societies

American Society of Composers, Authors and Publishers (ASCAP)

ASCAP is the largest organization in the US representing close to 400,000 artists. Members of ASCAP include publishers of music, composers and singers among many others. Perhaps the most admirable thing about this organization is that it is run solely by its members who are therefore aware of the problems and aspirations of fellow artists and this makes it the ideal organization for a independent musicians. ASCAP has a long history and covers all genres of music. Whether you plan on playing rock as a budding artist or jazz, reggae, gospel, Latin or any other kind of music, ASCAP has members who will offer you direction. Many famous big names are members of ASCAP. Examples include Stevie Wonder, Outkast, Madonna and Beyoncé.

At ASCAP, composition and performance of music is treated strictly as a business and the organization exists to help members benefit from their music business. It has a wide network, which ensures that as many music-playing outlets are licensed and this translates to huge revenues. ASCAP prides itself as the leading collector of license fees in the world. All the money collected is paid as royalty to its members after deduction of a little amount to cover for administrative expenses. The amount that the artist gets is usually close to 90% of the amount collected.

As an independent musician who intends to market and sell music online, ASCAP is especially ideal as it also issues licenses for websites. The organization has invested in advanced technology that enables it to protect copyrights online. Members of ASCAP enjoy a very comprehensive list of benefits. Holders of ASCAP's Careington Health Discount Card are entitled to discounts on their medical bills, which sometimes go as high as 60%.

By joining ASCAP, a budding musician can immediately register his songs and could soon be collecting royalties. To join ASCAP, a new member pays a non-refundable fee of $35 but this is all that the organization will take from you, as there are no annual subscriptions. ASCAP also works very effectively outside the US by collaborating with similar organizations abroad to monitor royalties due to its members from performances abroad. With affiliates globally, ASCAP effectively covers its members from the possibility of lost royalty income.

National Music Publishers Association (NMPA)

NMPA is a US-based organization whose prime duty is the protection of the rights of music creators. The organization actively watches out to make sure that royalties due to its members are paid and, should litigation become necessary, a member is assured of adequate representation. NMPA has considerable history behind it and this gives credibility to its ability to fight for the rights of its members. The association was formed in 1917, and in 1927 the association established an agency that was mandated to act as the monitoring arm to effectively handle matters of copyright licensing and generally act as a clearinghouse. This subsidiary, the Harry Fox Agency (HFA), is very active today to ensure that NMPA members get adequately compensated for their efforts.

The range of licenses it issues is broad and it covers both digital and mechanical users of music in the US. To join NMPA, you will need to be resident in the US and to have been actively involved in music publishing for at least one year. Moreover, the association needs to confirm that the applicant has an office in the US. Other requirements that a new applicant has to meet are the payment of $100 on application and a similar amount each year in membership. The association encourages those seeking to be admitted as new members to seek affiliation with its subsidiary, the HFA, but this is not a condition for registration. Working with an association like the NMPA is greatly beneficial for a new music publisher who might need a long period of time to know what goes on in the music industry.

Obtaining a license from the copyright office when you operate independently can be quite troublesome mainly because of bureaucratic processes that are time wasting and also because you will be required to make monthly accounting reports. When you work with NMPA's subsidiary, the HFA, you will only be required to make quarterly reports. HFA also offers a good compensation rate. A board of 17 members runs NMPA. Close to a century's experience that the company has in the promotion of music and the protection of the rights of music publishers should give any publisher confidence in the association's ability to expand their business.

Broadcast Music Incorporated (BMI)

BMI is a leading collector of license fees for composers, songwriters and publishers. Perhaps the biggest indicator of the huge profile that the company has is the vast number of superstar artists it represents. High-profile artists such as the late Michael Jackson, the Spice Girls, Kirk Franklin, Kanye West, Eminem, the Pussycat Dolls, and Tim McGraw are all represented by BMI. The total number of compositions that BMI represents is close to seven million and, since the music scene is very dynamic, that number keeps growing.

The history of BMI goes back to 1939 when the organization was created by a group of radio executives who wanted to assist musicians who were not covered by the performing rights organizations in existence then. The formation of BMI provided a lifeline for artists who specialized in blues, Latin, country and gospel since they did not have a representative. Today, the association covers music of all genres both in the US and globally.

Musicians represented by BMI have consistently won the industry's most prestigious awards and the only association that comes close is ASCAP. No other association has as many artists winning Grammys, CMAs, and R&R Hall of Fame and R&B Foundation awards. This is a good enough reason for a talented musician to consider joining the association.

A musician represented by BMI has immediate access to a vast resource pool. The association organizes frequent showcases and sponsors several genre-specific workshops. Some of the most outstanding workshops include the BMI Songwriters' Workshop, the Jazz Composers' Workshop, the Lehman Engel Musical Theater Workshop, and the Sundance Film Composers' workshop. Musicians represented by BMI enjoy good and affordable insurance covering both their health and instruments and also obtain discounts when they purchase the tools of the trade. BMI has reciprocal agreements with copyright organizations globally which helps to ensure that royalties due to musicians it represents are collected. Global collections from such associations are in excess of $200 million annually.

Joining BMI is unbelievably easy. Songwriters can join online and the process takes only a couple of minutes. Where most associations charge a joining fee, BMI does not but it requires that the musician signs a two-year contract. The vast resource pool and the history of BMI make the organization a prudent choice for all you talented up and coming musicians.

Performing Right Society & Mechanical Copyright Protection Society (PRS/MCPS)

PRS/MCPS is a non-profit royalty collection society set up to collect and pay royalties to record labels, composers, performers and songwriters when their music is sold. It was formerly known as the Performing Right Society and later together with the Mechanical-Copyright Protection Society formed the MCPS-PRS alliance in 1997. The society's deducts an administration fee from the money collected before distributing the reminder of the earnings to its members. The MCPS-PRS alliance is a huge society with over 60,000 members. It is the only society in the UK that independently funds upstart musicians through the PRS for Music Foundation. To date, this foundation has given over £13 million and funded over 4,000 music projects over a ten-year period. You can join PRS/MCPS as either a writer or a publisher. The society defines writers as people who have created an original song, lyrics or musical notations. To qualify for membership, the writer will need to prove that the music he composed has been broadcasted on TV or radio, has been used online, performed in a concert, or has been played in public.

To join the society as a publisher, you will need to meet similar requirements. Admission fees vary slightly between PRS and MCPS. Writers and publishers seeking MCPS membership are required to pay £50. To join PRS, the society requires writers to pay £10 while it demands £400 from those seeking admission as publishers. PRS and MCPS do not charge yearly membership fees. Becoming a member of PRS and MCPS is very beneficial and is highly recommended for any independent songwriter, rapper, MC, music producer, record label or music publisher. Members receive a quarterly magazine that is loaded with info crucial to the music industry. The societies also organize regular workshops, seminars and networking sessions. The MCPS-PRS alliance is networked with similar societies in over 100 countries ensuring that royalties due to members are collected globally, fast and accurately. The organization has also managed to negotiate discount deals for its members with several companies enabling their members to access external goods and services at discounted prices. Some of these deals include a 25% discount on medical cover with the BupaCare scheme and a 25% discount on handcrafted speakers from AUX.

Phonographic Performance Limited (PPL)

PPL is a London-based not-for-profit organization that collects and distributes public performance, performance over new media such as Internet radio stations or through websites and airplay royalties on behalf of record labels. The society ensures that they get their fair share of income from anybody who plays their music. A musician who is just starting out and has his or her music out there must fully understand that anybody who plays their music commercially needs to pay for it. Public places such as restaurants and pubs cannot play music without being properly licensed and this is where PPL comes in. Any organization that plays music without a license does so illegally and companies such as PPL could institute legal action against such organizations.

A brief history of PPL helps to shed light on why an independent musician needs to join this organization. PPL was formed through the amalgamation of two companies, EMI and Decca. EMI was instrumental in the creation of music copyright laws that are in operation in the UK today. In a landmark case in 1933, EMI successfully sued the owner of a Bristol restaurant who had been playing music without the permission of the copyright owners. This suit led to the establishment of the law necessitating the acquisition of a license to play any artist's music. While an independent musician has the legal right to get paid by those playing their music commercially, keeping track of the exact number of places the music is played is practically impossible. When you look at the proliferation of FM radio stations, the ever-growing number of TV stations and the innumerable online locations where music is available, the task of keeping track is not just immense but completely impossible for a single person, hence the need to join an organization like PPL.

PPL issues licenses to the various companies that play the music of the artists it represents. These organizations include radio and TV stations, Internet web portals as well as bars, restaurants and pubs. The company has a huge presence in the UK and also internationally and is able to collect license fees in more than twenty-four other countries. The license fees collected are then allocated and paid to musicians the company represents. Since this is a not-for-profit organization, it only deducts a little money to cover administrative expenses and the rest is shared among its members.

Society of European Stage Authors and Composers (SESAC)

A German immigrant, Paul Heinecke, formed SESAC in the United States in 1930 to help artists in Europe obtain royalties due to them from the American markets. Today SESAC is a respected association representing some of the leading music composers and publishers. Some of the most publicly visible artists that SESAC represents include Christina Aguilera and Justin Timberlake. Some of Hollywood's top film and TV music composers are also affiliated to SESAC, including Jonathan Wolff (composer of the music for "Will & Grace") and Dennis Brown ("Still Standing").

To help the musicians it represents get exposure and also to reward excellence, the association has a number of awards. One of these is the SESAC Jazz Music Awards, which is held in New York every year and which rewards SESAC musicians whose jazz music has received significant airplay during the year. Other awards include the SESAC Nashville Awards, SESAC New York Awards, SESAC Christian Music Awards, and the SESAC TV/Film Music Awards.

Compared to the other main PROs in the US (BMI & ASCAP), SESAC is a smaller association but it prides itself in offering a more personalized service to the musicians it represents. Musicians affiliated to SESAC enjoy benefits including discounts on subscription to the leading music industry journals such as *American Songwriter* and *Billboard* and discounts on music instrument courses through an arrangement made between SESAC and Legacy Learning Systems. For a budding musician who wishes to make and sell music online, the MasterWriter songwriting software is a must-have and SESAC affiliates get it at a 30% discount. Other benefits that musicians affiliated with SESAC enjoy include the Songwriter's Boot Camp, a free symposium where artists get to interact with main players in the industry. The association is selective in affiliating writers and publishers but encourages budding artists to contact an office representative to learn about the affiliation process. The association mainly aims to work with people pursuing music professionally but a budding musician has nothing to lose by contacting the association.

Sound Exchange

Sound Exchange is a not-for-profit organization that was formed in the US in 2003 and is mandated to collect royalties for copyright owners. It exclusively deals with royalties from the digital market and should therefore be of interest to a budding musician who wishes to produce music using digital means. Despite the short time it has been in existence, the organization today represents close to 4,000 record companies and thousands of new artists as well as the major labels. A board of directors that includes representatives from the major music labels governs Sound Exchange including SONY BMG, Universal Music Group, EMI, and Time Warner, and also representatives from independent labels. Artists' representatives are also drawn from other organizations representing musicians.

The organization does not collect royalties from public performances through the traditional media (radio and TV) but it is has exclusive collection rights for collection of royalties from satellite TV services and digital cable as well as satellite radio services. The organization also does not collect royalties for downloads as these are collected directly by the artist or the record company. Sound Exchange has been granted the powers to collect royalties from the digital world by the US Copyright office.

While it is possible for an artist today to get royalty payments for digital performances, this is a recent development in the US because as recently as 1995 there was no law in the country governing this and copyright owners were not getting paid for the public performance of their recordings. Things changed in 1995 when the Digital Performance in Sound Recording Act was passed. This Act together with the Digital Millennium Copyright Act of 1998 requires that the copyright owner get paid for music transmitted through digital means. The road to obtaining compensation for music makers has therefore been treacherous, so all digital content owners should take advantage of the new structures, which guard against the possible loss of deserved income.

The functions performed by Sound Exchange are different from those performed by the other main associations (SESAC, ASCAP & BMI) because these other organizations collect royalties for the owners of a song while Sound Exchange collects royalties for the recording. Sound Exchange should not therefore be viewed as being in competition with the other bodies. Every budding musician should join Sound Exchange. The organization does not charge any membership fees and only makes deductions for its administrative expenses from royalties collected.

Musicians Union (MU)

An interesting but true story is told about how the Musician's Union came into existence. Legend has it that an anonymous letter was circulated inviting the musicians in Manchester, UK, for a meeting to form a Protection Union. When the meeting eventually took place, the writer of the anonymous letter turned out to be a musician, Joe Williams, and he challenged fellow musicians to form a Union that would protect them from unscrupulous employers and amateurs. That meeting took place in May 1893 and by November of the same year the Amalgamated Musicians' Union (AMU) was launched with 1,000 members.

MU today is a respected leader in the music business representing over 32,000 musicians and handling all genres of music. It assists musicians in negotiating contracts, gives advice on copyright protection, and has full-time employees who deal with any issues their members have. Its members include well-established musicians as well as music students, and this makes it worth contacting for an independent musician.

The MU's national office is located in London but it has a full presence in the UK with regional offices in Cardiff, Manchester, Glasgow, and Birmingham. The company can also be reached online. Admission fees to the MU are based on a musician's earnings. A musician who earned more than £16,000 in the year preceding the date of application for membership will be required to pay £23 per month or £276 for the whole year. Those who earned less than 16,000 are required to pay £13 per month or £156 for the whole year. The MU also admits music students into the organization. In appreciation of the fact that the student probably has not made any income from their music, the organization only asks for £6.50 per month or £78 per year from student applicants as membership fees.

Joining MU will certainly help any budding musician, as there are many benefits that the organization's members enjoy. Apart from joining a modern and vibrant society, such a musician will benefit from a strong network of people who are interested in his career development. Courses, seminars and workshops to sharpen the student musician's skills are frequently organized by the MU.

The Association of Independent Music Publishers (AIMP)

AIMP is an organization that serves independent music publishers as well as those affiliated with other companies. Started in Los Angeles in 1977, the association has shown tremendous growth over the years and today has offices in both Los Angeles and New York. The number of the members shows the strength of this association in its online register that currently stands at close to 800.

The association's stated aim is to provide education and information on the latest trends in the music industry. This the association does by providing a forum through which members get to discuss issues affecting the industry and also informing and educating members on the most recent trends and changes in the industry. To facilitate member interaction, AIMP has regular workshops and forums as well as monthly meetings. Through the various meetings and discussion forums, members are also made aware of changes in legislation that impact on their work. Such meetings also help in the developing of new relationships. AIMP has three levels of membership each of which has differing benefits for the member. The first membership tier is the Online Only Membership, which is acquired on the payment of a $60 annual fee.

Online only members benefit by obtaining access to the members-only section of AIMP's website and being allowed access to the network of members as well as the right to participate in discussion forums. Such a member is also allowed to advertise his events in AIMP's calendar section in addition to getting discounts on AIMP's merchandise and the association's partner products.

AIMP's second membership tier is known as Professional Membership and allows the member to enjoy all the benefits that an online only member enjoys but also bestows on such a member voting rights. Professional members participate in the election of the board of directors of their chapter; obtain rights to attend Professional Members-only events as well as invitation to the association's AGM among other benefits. For Professional Membership, the annual charges are $75 and $76 for New York and LA chapters respectively.

The Premier Professional Membership is the final tier in AIMP's membership program and its members get to enjoy all the rights and privileges of the preceding two tiers in addition to other benefits such as discounts on AIMP's events, luncheons and admission to the Premier members-only events. This membership costs $150 per year.

The German Musical Performing and Mechanical Reproduction rights Society (GEMA)

GEMA is a German acronym, which stands for the Society for Musical Performing and Mechanical Reproduction rights. It is based in Berlin Germany and has a membership of over 60,000 in Germany alone and more than a million other members internationally. GEMA has been in existence for over a hundred years. The society was founded in 1903 when two Germans, Richard Strauss and Friedrich Rosch, founded a co-operative society for German composers. This co-operative society, the GDT, later changed names and became GEMA. The society is run as a not-for-profit organization and on collection of license fees, it only deducts an administrative fee and distributes the rest of the collected amount to the members. With GEMA, an artist knows the kind of money to expect as the administration fee is not an arbitrary figure but a very specific percentage of the amount collected. Currently, the fee is 14.4%. Membership to GEMA is open to music composers, lyricists, and publishers, and the company differentiates between three kinds of membership: affiliate, extraordinary, and full membership. Affiliate membership can be obtained upon application and payment of an admission fee of EUR 51.13 for lyricists and composers. Additionally, affiliate members pay an annual subscription of EUR 25.56.

To be admitted as an extraordinary member, GEMA requires the applicant to submit original or photocopies of works that have been performed, broadcast, and distributed to the public in various forms such as audio and audiovisual. An extraordinary member of GEMA qualifies to full membership after five years. Apart from meeting the five-year waiting requirement, such members are supposed to meet certain earning requirements. For a lyricist, for example, GEMA requires that he or she generate an income of at least EUR 30,677.51 over the five-year period to qualify for full membership. Despite the varying membership requirements, each member obtains the same level of service from the organization and this is critical because a budding musician, who can only join GEMA as an affiliate member, would like assurances that his rights are fully taken care of. To benefit from copyright protection that GEMA offers its members, any artist who joins the association is required to notify the organization of their published works, especially those that are likely to generate income. This aids in monitoring and data collection. For people who perform in a band, they can join GEMA but only as individual members.

The Music Producers Guild (MPG)

The Music Producers Guild is one of the leading organizations fully dedicated to the promotion and protection of the interests of all players in the UK music industry. Its members include producers, programmers, mixers and engineers among other music production professionals.

MPG provides an excellent platform for any musician but is especially ideal for budding artists. The company's website is loaded with tons of information on the company and its members but there is one feature that could work miracles for a new musician. Members are allowed to announce the projects they are currently undertaking under "members' current project." This link allows for serious networking in addition to providing useful information on what projects are likely to succeed. In addition, it creates a competitive environment and offers upstarts the chance to meet with more established players. Joining the MPG also offers the new member an immense range of benefits. Members receive a free copy the MPG Newsletter which is an authoritative publication covering all areas of the music industry. MPG is also affiliated to Association of Independent Music (AIM) and this enables MPG members to receive a 50% joining fee reduction when they join AIM. Other benefits include preferential rates on equipment rentals through an arrangement made between MPG and FX Rentals as well as a free 30-minute consultation with Penny Ganz, a leading music business lawyer. Most of the benefits are only available to full members of the company.

MPG has two types of memberships. To acquire Full membership, one is required to pay 120 sterling pounds per year in addition to meeting some music industry knowledge and production requirements. The applicant needs to have six credits for engineering, production, mixing, or any other activity connected with the production of music that has subsequently been released and is available through traditional outlets. Alternatively, the applicant will qualify if he has received 12 credits for music available through digital download. Full membership gives the MPG member many benefits including free entry to all MPG events and discounts on tickets to MPG Awards. A full member is also able to vote in the selection of the shortlist for the MPG Awards. The second kind of membership with MPG is Associate membership for which an applicant is required to pay 55 sterling pounds per year. While the benefits due to associate members are limited, it is still a good place for independent musicians.

The Music Publishers Association (MPA)

The history of the Music Publishers Association (MPA) dates back to the nineteenth century. If a single company in the music industry could boast that it has seen it all, that company would be MPA. The issues that led to the formation of this company were as relevant in that century as they are today. Nine music publishers formed MPA in 1881. These publishers were concerned that the copyright laws in operation then were not adequate to protect the works of artists. In nineteenth-century UK, copyright issues were governed by the Copyright Act 1842 but this act was deficient because it did not specify penalties for copyright fraud. Aggrieved publishers could only institute civil actions against such offenders in the hope of obtaining injunctions and probably damages. The aim of the MPA from the very outset was to deal with situations such as those occasioned by the deficient Act and to protect the music publishing industry. It aimed to do this by lobbying the government locally, internationally and in the British colonies. The MPA started as a group of nine music publishers and by 1887 had opened an office in London. This long history is evidence enough that MPA has the kind of copyright protection knowledge that other companies can only dream about. The immense technological changes that our society has gone through over the years, while being beneficial to the larger society, have also presented wonderful opportunities for fraudsters and ever-increasing challenges to music publishers.

Today, MPA has a membership of about 250 publishers. The publisher who joins MPA knows he is dealing with a serious company because, apart from its enviable history, the company is the UK's ISMN agency.

ISMN refers to the numbering system used for printed music (similar to ISBN on printed books). To assist newcomers to the music industry, the company offers the MPA Induction course four times each year and conducts regular seminars where experts offer advice and guidance on all publishing issues. Members of MPA enjoy a huge range of benefits including free job ad spaces in the company's website as well as discounted subscriptions to the industry's leading publications such as *Billboard* and *Classical Music*. Up-and-coming music entrepreneurs who need the helping hand of a true veteran and certified fighter, perhaps you need not look any further than the MPA.

The British Phonographic Industry (BPI)

BPI was formed in 1973 with the stated objective of representing the record industry in the UK in negotiations with unions and the government and to promote the welfare of artists. From humble beginnings, this company has grown over the years and today has a membership of over 400. At BPI, you will find both independent music companies as well as the major labels. To achieve its objective of promoting British music and to ensure that its members thrive, BPI offers it members very comprehensive support. All members have access to a huge source of statistics relevant to the industry and the company organizes regular training courses and seminars. The company's legal department offers critical legal advice on a musician's relationships with the company and other music bodies such as the Musician's union.

As a leading player in the music industry, the company lobbies the government to improve the conditions of musicians. BPI organizes the annual BRIT Awards. This is a huge platform that helps promote new musicians as well as reward excellence. For a new artist, getting nominated for this award easily turns a career around. Each year also, the company produces the BPI Statistical Handbook, which, among others, contains information on record sales in the UK.

This handbook provides almost everything you will ever need to know about the UK music industry. Critical information in the handbook that a budding musician cannot afford to ignore includes analyses of record sales by genre as well as buying trends. From this handbook you will get to know which demographic group buys which music and the average amounts spent on music. Comparative data on music sales over a ten-year period is also provided. To help it members penetrate the lucrative international market, especially the US and Japan, BPI organizes networking events through international media partners. New musicians are trained and mentored on ways of developing their music to make it achieve international acclaim. BPI has two kinds of membership. Full membership, which is open to companies that own or license UK recording copyrights, currently cost £67.50 plus 5% PPL distribution payment plus VAT. The second category of membership is Associate Membership. This is for companies that do not own or exclusively license British music. The joining fee is £500 plus VAT.

The Association of Independent Music (AIM)

AIM is based in the UK and was established with the intention of assisting independent record companies and distributors. With a membership of 850 members, this association controls a substantial portion of the UK music market. Regardless of the kind of music a budding musician plays, AIM will be able to assist as it handles copyright issues for artists of all genres. An outstanding service that AIM offers that should especially appeal to upstarts in the music industry is its mentorship scheme. Independent labels get to enjoy the association's support through a program that puts them in touch with well-established players in the industry and who therefore help them develop. This is a very important scheme because the beginning of a music career can be totally terrifying and many give up after just a few days. The budding musician also gets to benefit from a thoroughly developed network, which puts the musician in touch with other recording companies.

AIM members have access to a members-only website which is full of important info and they are frequently updated on the latest developments in the industry via email. Advice on how to run an independent label is provided immediately you register with this association through a free e-book. To assist the increasing number of artists who sell their music online, the association has an affiliate company known as AIM Digital, which was created to specifically negotiate online music production and distribution deals. The company observes the latest developments in the digital world and communicates this to its members.

In addition, it runs an affiliate program that enables it to negotiate deals for its members outside the UK. Membership to AIM is open to recording companies that are based in the UK. Such companies need to show evidence that they own copyright to distribute recordings or make sound recordings. The admission fee is £100 plus VAT and an annual subscription fee of £120. The annual fee for distribution companies is a bit higher at £750 plus VAT. AIM waives the joining fees to companies, which are members of certain organization with which it has collaborative links. Some of the organizations whose members are exempt from this admission fee include BASCA, the Music Publishers Association (MPA), Armstrong Learning and the Welsh Music Foundation (WMF). By joining AIM, music entrepreneurs will benefit from a vast resource pool that could help turn a career around.

CHAPTER SEVEN

Producing Your Presentation

"They expect a professional presentation, so they expect to see a "professional." Dress appropriately for the occasion, but don't be one of the crowd."

— Wess Roberts

Elevator Pitch

"Luck is a matter of preparation meeting opportunity."

— Oprah Winfrey

An elevator pitch is a clear and concise description about your business so straightforward that a child is able to understand what your business is about by the time you reach the ground floor. Just imagine you attended a seminar or a concert and whilst going to the bathroom you happen to bump into Russell Simmons or Percy "Master P" Miller, both of whom are known for investing in young talent. What would you say? How would you approach them? And how would you get them to take you seriously?

This is where an elevator pitch comes in handy. You need to be ready to seize any opportunity for investment, and therefore a well-planned and religiously practiced pitch is the key.

An elevator pitch is completely different from a sales pitch. The core purpose is not to sell your products to the listener but to paint a picture in the minds of the listener of the business opportunity emphasizing what's in it for them using unambiguous language. Your elevator pitch should answer six key questions on behalf of the listener. The questions are as follows:

1. What is your product or service?

2. Who is your core target audience/market?

3. How will the business make its money (business model)?

4. Who are the management?

5. Who are the direct competitors?

6. What are your main unique selling points/competitive advantages?

The structure of your elevator pitch should include four key elements. These are as follows:

The Hook

This is how you will win the attention of your listener. You need to first get them interested to begin with. This could be a brave question or an enticing statement.

Length of time

You may be lucky enough to be given a few moments of their time. Your elevator pitch should be approximately 60 seconds and no more. It should answer all the six important questions mentioned above too.

Passion

If you don't come across as passionate then your chances of getting their attention will be small. You must always transmit positive energy when talking about your business venture.

Request

At the end of your elevator pitch always make some form of request weather it's asking for their contacts details, scheduling a date for a full presentation, or any referrals or recommendations.

Business Presentations

"It takes one hour of preparation for each minute of presentation time."

— Wayne Burgraff

A presentation is essential for communicating business propositions. If you decide to approach investors or intend to go into partnership with another business, you will almost certainly need to present your ideas, aims, and objectives to these individuals, groups or organizations in a way that will persuade, convince, and get the results you require. To do so, you must fully understand exactly what an effective business presentation should entail and the best way to structure you presentation. Before you start to work on your presentation you should ask your self a set of questions so that you can capture all the elements needed for success.

Below is a series of questions you should answer before you start to produce your presentation.

- What do I want to achieve from this presentation?
- Who will I be presenting to?
- Where will my presentation take place?
- What equipment will I need to deliver my presentation effectively?
- What materials will I need to deliver my presentation effectively?

- What software should I use, and would it be compatible with the any PC?

- What are the main points I need to make?

- What information will I need to research and gather?

- What style will I use, formal or informal?

- Who will I be working with?

- How much time will I have?

- What sort of questions should I prepare for?

When you start to construct your presentation bear in mind that people attend presentations to gain new or valuable information, learn something, or explore the possibility of opportunity. Effective presentations will grab the attention of the audience and encourage them to ask questions. In order to get what you want from your listeners you must first give them what they want. The key is to get their attention from the onset and then grab it again every time you want to emphasize a point. In addition, you should try to involve your audience in your presentations, as it will enhance your mission to persuade them.

Below are some necessary strategies to structure your presentation.

Strategic Approach

Always remember that people attend presentations to gain new or valuable information, learn something, or explore the possibility of an opportunity. Focus on your purpose and create ways to deliver your points effectively. It is all in the timing.

Emphasize the Benefits

What will your business offer? Will your presentation give someone in the audience a chance to own a share of the publishing copyrights of your publishing company or gain a return of a million dollars on a thirty-grand investment in just eighteen months!

Show Concern

Investors respect those who respect money, so indicating that you fully understand the risks involved with the music and entertainment industry will help shape and influence the concerns your listeners may have for the better. It is important to acknowledge that investors often fear problems and challenges, and that the initial investment required may call for further investment. This is a huge concern for investors and could prove to be a deal breaker. In effort to reduce these concerns, creating counter arguments backed up by facts and figures will help create a positive representation for your proposition.

Robustness and Credibility

In order for your audience to respect and take you seriously, you must demonstrate the soundness of your business and the credibility of your standing. The best and most appropriate strategies for doing so are to use persuasive techniques, industry knowledge, or experience, and any personal achievement.

Approaching Investors

O ne of the top reasons that new ventures fail is because they do not
have adequate funds to make it through the crucial start-up process. However, there is funding available out there to entrepreneurs who
are well prepared, organized and resourceful. All up-and-coming entertainment entrepreneurs who want to raise money for their new ventures
need to educate themselves and commit to the sometimes arduous but
rewarding road to funding.

Any venture seeking financing should have a properly prepared business
plan. There are many professionals who can prepare this document for
you. If you attempt to complete this on your own it is vital that you have
financial professionals review your plan before submitting it to potential
investors. You often are presented with only one chance to make a great
impression on investors and a poorly prepared business plan is an instant
red flag in the eyes of investors.

Friends and Family

As an aspiring entertainment entrepreneur you may not have the credentials to gain the trust of established investors and therefore may need to
look closer to home for support. Family and friends are often the way
most entrepreneurs get started in business. If you could loan a couple
hundred dollars or even a few thousand from your nearest or dearest

relatives in return for a reasonable share in the business, chances are they will also provide a helping hand in the management and business operations. Family and friends are always a good place to start providing you can trust them to be a part of your company.

Business Bank Loans

For those who qualify, a bank loan may be a source of funding. Banks, like private investors, are going to want to see a professional business plan with marketing, analysis, and most importantly, and solid financial projections and statements. Unless you have extensive experience creating financial forecasts this should be left to a seasoned professional.

Government Funding

Opportunities for federal, state, or local grant funding of music-related projects exist primarily for 501(c)(3) non-profit organizations such as dance groups, orchestras, choral groups, and other community-based cultural charities. Individual musicians may, on rare occasions, be eligible for government grant funding.

State Grants

State governments offer grants to fund various music projects and programs. Some of the state agencies that offer grants include:

New York State Council on the Arts (NYSCA)

The NYSCA funds musicians, organizations, and radio and television programming. The organization aims to aid musicians give public performance in order to establish themselves in the field. Government grants are also awarded to non-profit organizations and creative projects that introduce brand new musical technologies and trends. However, there is a clause attached to this: all applicants must live in New York for a minimum of two years to qualify for these grants.

California Arts Council (CAC)

The council, in conjunction with the Department of Justice, funded 42 known art organizations in 2009. The aim was to help the organizations and societies support public performances in the field of music throughout the state.

Massachusetts Cultural Council (MCC)

The MCC offers annual grants to educational music programs that fund school trips, public performances, concerts and festivals in order to enrich individual and community life.

Investor Options

Angel Investors are typically high-net-worth individuals who became a success in business themselves. These investors provide capital and business expertise for an equity share in the company. Typical investment amounts start as low as $25,000 and into the low seven-figures.

American Angel Networks: Finding the right angel investor could help you get your start-up off the ground. Angel-investor networks are a good place to start looking for funding.

European Angel Networks: Gate2Growth is a pan-European business platform for entrepreneurs seeking financing, investors, incubator managers, knowledge transfer offices, and academics. http://www.gate2growth.com

European Business Angels Network (EBAN) is the European trade association for business angel networks. http://www.eban.org.

UK Angel Networks: The British Business Angels Association (BBAA) is the National Trade Association for the UK's Business Angel Networks and the early stage investment market and is backed by the Department for Business, Enterprise and Regulatory Reform. http://www.bbaa.org.uk/.

Venture Capitalists (VCs) are a great option for firms that have already begun accepting orders and are looking for a sizable investment to take their business to the next level. VCs generally lend in the millions and are always looking for the next great business to get involved in. If your business is a start-up with no earnings then this is not the place to begin your search, but there are cases where VC firms have been willing to invest millions in the right teams with the right ideas.

Entrepreneur.com presents an annual list of the top VC firms
http://www.entrepreneur.com/vc100

CHAPTER EIGHT

Making it Happen

"Some people want it to happen, some wish it would happen, others make it happen."

— *Michael Jordan*

Now that you have gained the knowledge and understanding behind the science of achieving success, it's your turn to make it happen. When doing so never forget that small successes lead to big successes. Systems and processes are the key factors for accomplishment. The main difference between successful entrepreneurs and unsuccessful entrepreneurs is that those who are product-oriented often fail. Never create a solution, product, or service without first identifying a problem, need, or want. Those who are market-oriented often hit upon success after they have spent time understanding the requirements of a marketplace and developing a solution, product, or service to satisfy that specific market. The same applies to music and entertainment entrepreneurs. Stay market focused and NOT product orientated. Always move with understanding into a marketplace and play close attention to other entrepreneurs who have been successful with similar ideas to yours, but do not copy or imitate their ideas.

Above anything else, business ventures must make financial sense. Do not make the same mistakes as many talented musicians who tried to go it independently but allowed their egos to dominate their activities. There is a thin line between ego and passion. It is your responsibility to stay focused and make sure that your energy is a passionate force rather than an egotistical one. Use your strengths as a starting point and try not to expose your weaknesses.

Most successful entrepreneurs would verify that building on their strengths and carefully managing their weaknesses (hence building first-class teams and work units) had enabled them to accomplish success with their business. In other words, where they were weak and lacked ability, a member in the team had those strengths and capabilities. Besides going for what you know, you should ensure that your business proposition is unique, distinctive, and very competitive. It is very important that you understand the fact that business success is dependent on establishing, developing, and sustaining a competitive advantage in the marketplace. Ask yourself, what benefits will your customers get when they buy from you? And how will you sustain these benefits to remain competitive?

Finally, do not rush things. You must learn to work with time, as time will be the greatest business partner you can ever have. Always move one step at a time with the assurance that the results that you are seeking are correct and are strategically planned. Do not attempt to do everything yourself. Build a good and well-organized management team and stay loyal to your work unit. History has shown that once millions of dollars get involved, many successful entrepreneurial teams, especially those in the urban music sectors such as Hip Hop, become enemies affecting the business. You must learn to break that cycle. Don't be another statistic.

Remember, the key factor for success in today's music and entertainment industry is content ownership. Don't just work for a paycheck signed by someone else. Produce and sell your own product. The asset that you create today could continue to produce income for you for the next five or ten or twenty years.

Good luck with you endeavors!

Music and Entertainment Industry Resources

The following information is presented to assist music industry entrepreneurs. While every attempt has been made to present accurate
information, the music industry evolves at a rapid pace. Check before
contacting any of these resources; the authors cannot be responsible for
errors or changes in contact information.

Music and Entertainment Industry

The old tried-and-tested activities of the music industry no longer apply
to today's digital music environment. Major labels are finding it difficult to keep up with the new developments. With the downturn in the
industry, independent musicians have gained the upper hand retaining
full ownership of their content, enabling them to license it to who ever
is paying. Furthermore, technological advances mean professional studios and expensive music producers are not essential to the unsigned
sector anymore. We have included in this final section some key industry contacts. These contacts could help you with sourcing venues when
planning events or gigs to promote yourself or an artist signed to your
company. Also included are publishers, established industry managers,
A&R representatives, and music producers.

What exactly is an A&R representative?

The initials A&R stand for "artists and repertoire." In the mid-twentieth century, A&R men were employed by major labels to oversee the careers of contracted talent. They handled everything from helping the artist select songs to hiring musicians for studio sessions. As artists became increasingly independent, the term evolved to mean someone employed by a record company to discover and acquire new talent.

Why will I need an A&R rep if I have my own music business?

As an independent you will most probably be the copyright owners of the content you wish to get out there. With this intellectual property you are able to earn income through selling the mechanical rights of your content to various established companies. These companies will then have your permission to manufacture and distribute the musical works in the agreed territories as mentioned in chapter six.

Your goal is to utilize as many channels as possible to deliver your content. For example, you could have three separate record companies working for you, getting your material to the markets, whilst you still remain the copyright owner of the content. When approaching an A&R rep, make sure that they work for a company that specifically deals with the market segment you intend to reach. In the package include any information about your company and emphasize the future benefits that they will receive if they decide to work with your company. Also include how much local or regional success you have already achieved, providing and images, press, and web links as physical evidence. Below is a comprehensive list of reputable A&R contact details in which you could use to target specific organization.

A&R of the United States (US)

Activate Entertainment
11054 Ventura Blvd. Ste 333, Studio City, CA 91604
Phone: 818 505 0669
Email: jay@2activate.com
Genres: Hip Hop, Rock, Sound track
A&R: Monique Hughes

Aftermath
2220 Colorado Blvd Santa Monica, CA 90404
Phone: 310 865 7642 Fax: 310 865 7068
Credits: The Game, Blackstreet, Dr. Dre, Eminem, Eve,
A&R: Andre Young/ Mike Lynn/Angelo Sanders

A&M Records
2220 Colorado Avenue Suite 1230 CA
90404 Santa Monica
Phone: 310 865 1000
Fax: 310 865 6270
A&R: Ron Fair/ Tony Ferguson

A&M / Octone Records NY
560 Broadway Suite 500 NY 10012 New York
Phone: 646 613 0200 Fax: 646 613 9096
www.octonerecords.com
bb@amoctone.com
Credits: Sheryl Crow, Black Eyed, Peas, Keyshia Cole, Pussycat Dolls
A&R: Ben Berkman

Amathus Music
P.O. Box 95, Hewlett, NY 11557
Email: amathusmusic@aol.com
Genres: Dance Music, Pop, Electronic
A&R: Chris Panaghi

American Recordings
9830 Wilshire Blvd.
Beverly Hills CA 90212-18045
Phone: 818 953 3392 or 818 953 3295
Antony.bland@wbr.com
Artists: Beastie Boys, Public Enemy, Run-D.M.C, Sir Mix-a-lot, Slayer,
System Of A Down
A&R: Rick Rubin/ Dino Paredes/ Antony Bland

Atlantic (WEA)
3400 W. Olive Ave. 3rd floor
Burbank, CA 91505
Phone: 818-238-6800
Email: mike.caren@atlanticrecords.com
www.atlantic-records.com
Artists: Drama, Nappy Roots, Sunshine Anderson, T.I., Trina, Twista,
Lil Kim
A&R:
Mike Caren/ John Rubeli/ Shawn Barron
Chris Morris: 818 238 6913
Danny Wimmer: Danny.wimmer@atlanticrecords.com

Atlantic Records (WEA)
1290 Ave. of the Americas 27th Fl.
New York, NY 10104
Phone: 212-707-2000
Phone: 212 707 2312
Fax: 212-405-5477
Julie.greenwald@atlanticrecords.com
www.atlantic-records.com
Artists: Freeway, Jay-Z, Cam'Ron, Death Cab For Cutie, Jewel, Maria
Carey, Fat Joe
A&R: Chris Foitle/ Darrale Jones/Rob Tewlow: Tel: 212 707 2312
Gee Roberson: G.roberson@atlanticrecords.com
Jimmy Bralower: Tel: 212 707 2312
JoJo Brim: Tel: 212 707 2312

ATO Records
44 Wall St. 22nd Floor
New York, NY 10005
www.atorecords.com
info@atorecords.com
A&R: Dave Matthews / Bruce Flohr

Bad Boy Entertainment
1710 Broadway 16th Floor
New York, NY 10018
Phone: 212 381 1540 Fax: 212 381 1599
www.badboyonline.com
Artists: Black Rob, Carl Thomas, Dream, Shyne, Dream, 112, Craig
Mack, Faith Evans, Jodeci
A&R: Harve Pierre/ Shannon Lawrence/Lindsay Rodman/ Daniel
Mitchell
Conrad Dimanche. Tel: 212 757 0808
Gwendolyn Niles: Gniles@badboyworldwide.com

Blackground Records
155 W 19th Street
New York, NY 10011
www.blackground.com
Artists: Aaliyah, R Kelly, JoJo
A&R: Barry Hankerson

Black Heart Records
636 Broadway
New York, NY 10012
212 353 9600
Email: blackheart@blackheart.com

Beat Club/ Mosley Music Group
6616 South Dixie Highway #377
FL 33143 Miami
Phone: 305 389 2053
Fax: 310 865 7908
Credits: Bubba Sparxxx
A&R:
Tim Mosley. Tel: 305 389 2053 Fax: 310 865 7908
Eric Spence. Eric.spence@mosleymusicgroup.net
www.mosleymusicgroup.net

Capitol Records (EMD)
1750 N. Vine St. 10th Fl
Hollywood, CA 90028
Phone: 323-462-6252
Web: www.hollywoodandvine.com
Artists: Chingy, Dilated Peoples, Marcy Playground,
A&R: Darius Jones/ Marc Nathan/ Jaime Feldman/ Steve Prudholme
/ Wendy Goldstein

Capitol Nashville (EMD)
3322 W. End Ave. 11th Fl.
Nashville, TN 37203
Phone: 615-269-2000
Submission Line: 615 269 2075
A&R: Larry Willoughby/Autumn House/ Mellissa Fuller
A&R@emicap.com

Columbia (Sony)
2100 Colorado Ave.
Santa Monica, CA 90404
Phone: 310-449-2100
Fax: 310-449-2071
Artists: Crazy Town, Offspring
www.columbiarecords.com
A&R:Matt Pinfield/ Jay Landers/ Marshall Altman

Columbia (Sony)
550 Madison Ave. 24th Fl.
New York, NY 10022
Phone: 212-833-4000 Fax: 212-833-4389
www.sony.com/music/columbia
Credits: Joss Stone, Goodie Mob, Outkast, Pink, Usher, Youngbloodz,,
Maxwell, Nas
A&R
John Doelp. Tel: 212 833 4623
Simon Collins. Tel: 646 436 8744
Kevin Patrick/ Mitchell Cohen/ Steve Lillywhite / Steve Barnett/
Steve Berkowitz/
Don Devito: Don.devito@sonymusic.com)

Def Jam Recordings
PO Box 78386
Atlanta, GA 30357
Phone: 212 333 8000
www.defjamsouth.net
Credits: Ludacris, Scarface
A&R: Brad Jordan/ DJ Khaled

Disturbing Tha Peace
1451 Woodmont Lane NW Suite A
29th floor
Atlanta, GA 30318
Phone: 404 351 7387 Fax: 404 351 7168
www.dtprecords.com
Credits: Bobby Valentino, Chingy, Lil Flip
A&R
Ken Bailey/ Sean Taylor/ Erica Novich
Alamo: Alamodtp@gmail.com

D'Mar Entertainment
7723 Tylers Place Blvd. Ste. 275
West Chester, OH 45069
Email: dmarentertainment@fuse.net
Genres: Smooth Jazz, Gospel, R&B
A&R: Sheila A. Jordan

Downtown Music
485 Broadway, 3rd Floor
New York NY 10013
Phone: 212 625 2980
www.downtownmusic.com
info@downtownmusic.com
Credits: Gnarls Barkley, Jason Mraz, Third Eye Blind, Vitamin C
A&R: Josh Deutsch

Elektra Entertainment/ Atlantic
3400 W. Olive Ave. 2nd Floor
Burbank, CA 91505
Phone: 818-238-6800
www.electra.com
Artists: Missy Elliott, Lil Mo, Tweet, Yolanda Adams, T.I., Twista,
Trina,
A&R: Mike Caren/ John Rubeli/ Chris Morris

Elektra (WEA)/ Atlantic
1290 Ave of the Americas
24th Floor
New York, NY 10104
Phone: 212-707-2000 Fax: 212-405-5411
Artists: Fabolous, Lil Mo, Kanye West
A&R:
Leigh Lust/ Darrale Jones/
Kenya.simon@atlanticrecords.com
Gee Roberson. Tel: 212 707 2312

Geffen Records
2220 Colorado Ave. 4th Floor
Santa Monica, CA 90404
Phone: 310-865-1000
Fax: 310-865-7069
Credits: Common, Slim Thug, The Roots, Talib Kweli
A&R: Thom Panunzio/ Jordan Schur/ Earl Johnson

Interscope Records/ Geffen
2220 Colorado Avenue 5th Floor
Santa Monica CA 90404
Phone: 310 865 1000 Fax: 310 865 7908
www.interscope.com
Credits: 50 Cent, Mobb Depp, Gwen Stefani, M.I.A.
A&R: Jenn Littleton / /Tony Ferguson/Luke Wood. Tel: 310 865 7713

Island — Def Jam Music Group
825 8th Ave. 28th Flr.
New York, NY 10019
Phone: 212-333-8000 Fax: 212 333 7255
Credits: Ne-Yo, Rihanna, Pink, Def Squad, Musiq Soulchild, DMX,
Busta Rhymes, LL Cool J, Lionel Richie, Kanye West, Jay-Z, Nas,
Rick Ross, Young Jeezy
A&R: Karen Kwak/Tyran Smith/Joshua Sarubin/ Karen Kwak

Jazz & Classics EMI Records
Blue Note, Narada Jazz. Metro Blue
150 5th Ave New York, NY10010
Phone: 212 786 8600 Fax: 212 786 8668
Credits: Akon, Remy Ma, Terror Squad, Melissa Young Cash
A&R: Bruce Lundvall/ Eli Wolf/ Lorne Behram/ Keith Karwelies

JIVE RECORDS
550 Madison Ave 13th Floor
New York, NY 10022
Phone 212 833 8000
Email: peter.thea@sonybmg.com
www.jiverecords.com
Credits: Chris Brown, Ciara Donell, Jones, Britney Spears, Backstreet
Boys, Justin Timberlake, Nsync, Pink, Petey, Pablo, Three Days Grace
A&R: Toi Green/ David Lighty / Larry Campbell
Wayne Williams. Tel: 212 824 1307
Mickey Wright. Tel: 212 727 0016
Barry Weiss. Tel: 212 833 8000
Mark Pitts. Tel: 212 833 6500

J Records
745 5th.Ave 6th Flr.
New York, NY 10151
Phone: 646-840-5600
www.j-records.com
Credits: Alicia Keys, Angie Stone, Dido, Santana,Whitney Houston,
Monica, O-Town, Rubin Studdard, Tyrese, Ruben Studdard, Kelly
Clarkson
A&R:
Rani Hancock/Clive Davis/ Peter Edge/ Larry Jackson/ Stephen Fer-
rera

Koch
740 Broadway 7th Floor
New York, NY 10003
Phone: 212 353 8800 Fax: 212 228 0660
Email: cliff.cultreri@kochent.com
A&R
Cliff Cultreri: cliff.cultreri@kochent.com
Laurel Dann: laurel.dann@kochent.com

Lil Jon/ BME
2144 Hills Avenue N.W. Suite D2
Atlanta, GA 30318
Phone: 404 367 8130 Fax: 404 367 8630
Credits: Lil Scrappy, Lil Jon & The East Side Boyz
A&R: Dewayne Searcy/ Rob McDowell/Vincent Phillips
marmstrong@bmerecordings.com

Priority Records (EMD)
1750 N. Vine St. Suite 900
Hollywood, CA 90028
Phone: 323-462-6252 Fax: 323-469-4542
www.priorityrecords.com
A&R: Steve Prudholme / Kevin Faist

Purple Ribbon
684 Antone Street Atlanta GA 30318
Phone: 404 350 3332 Fax: 404 350 3208
www.outkast.com
Credits: Outkast
A&R: Regina Davenport

Republic Records
1755 Broadway 6th Floor
New York NY 10019
Phone: 212 841 5100 Fax: 212 841 8012
www.republicrecords.com
Credits: Baby Bash, Chamillionaire,
A&R: Avery Lipman/ Tom Mackay

Shady Records
151 Lafayette Street 6th Floor
New York, NY 10013
Phone: 212 324 2410 Fax: 212 324 2415
www.shadyrecords.com
Credits: Eminem, D12, 50 Cent
A&R: Marc Labelle/ Riggs Morales

So So Def
1350 Spring Street Suite 750 Atlanta, GA 30309
Phone: 404 888 9900 Fax: 404 888 9901
www.sosodef.net
Bow Wow, Da Brat, Kris Kross
A&R: Eddie Weathers

Star Trak Entertainment
825 8th Ave 29th Fl
New York NY 10019
Phone: 212 333 8000 Fax: 212 603 1981
www.startrakmusic.com
Artists: Neptunes, Clipse
A&R: Rob Walker: Robert.walker@startrakmusic.com

Street Records Corp
1755 Broadway 6th
New York NY 10019
Phone: 212 331 2628 Fax: 212 331 2620
www.srcrecords.net
Credits: Akon, Syren, David Banner, Wu Tang
A&R
Gaby Acevedo: Gordonj@srcmusic.net
Jason Kpana: Srcrecords@gmail.com
Jamaal Meeks: Srcrecords@gmail.com
Steve Rifkind Srcrecords@gmail.com

Tommy Boy
902 Broadway 13th Floor
NY, New York 10010
Phone: 212-388-8300
Fax: 212-388-8400
www.tommyboy.com
A&R: Tom Silverman

TVT Records
23 East 4th Street 3rd Floor
New York, NY 10003
Phone 212-979-6410 Fax 212-979-6489
www.tvtrecords.com
info@tvtrecords.com
Credits: Lil Jon & The East Side Boyz, Ying Yang Twins
A&R
Leonard B Johnson/ Jennifer O'Neill / Steve Gottlieb/ James Eichel-
berger

Universal (UMG)
1755 Broadway, 7th Floor
New York, NY 10019
Phone: 212-373-0600 Fax: 212-373-0688
www.universalrecords.com
Credits: Ali, Nelly, St. Lunatics, 702,
No Unsolicited Material
A&R
Avery Lipman/ Kevin Law/ Bruce Carbone/
Anthony Rollo. Tel: 212 841 8231
Anthony.rollo@umusic.com
Sal Guastella Direct Line: (616 212 8418)

VP RECORDS
89-05 138th Street
Jamaica NY 11435
Phone: 718 425 1138 Fax: 718 658 3573
www.vprecords.com
Credits: Sean Paul, Joel Chin
A&R
Murray Elias: Melias1000@aol.com
Joel Chin. Tel: 718 291 7058 Fax: 718 658 3573
information@vprecords.com

Warner Bros.
3300 Warner Blvd. 3rd Floor.
Burbank, CA 91505
Phone: 818 846 9090 Fax: 818 953 3423
Credits: Disturbed, Faith Hill
No Unsolicited Material
A&R
Eric Lobato: Eric.lobato@atlspecialops.com
David Foster. Tel: 818 953 3377 or David.foster@wbr.com
Craig Aaronson Craig.aaronson@wbr.com

Music Producers

Below is a comprehensive list of some of the world's greatest music producers. If you write great songs then you can set up your own publishing company and explore a joint venture with any one of these listed producers to create hit songs. When approaching these producers you should send them no more than three samples of your work, and you need to transmit your vision of any anticipated outcomes.

Producers such as Timbaland are always on the lookout for great songwriters. Remember it's all about instilling a compelling vision of the end results. If they can see what it is you anticipate, then that is all you need to take your music to the next level. The good news to working with an established producer is that if a music producer receives your vision and believes in your work, you may not have to pay any upfront fees for their services. This is where you will need to negotiate on the contract terms and conditions. The other good thing is that these music producers know and have business relationships with top people in the industry, which would also be a huge advantage for your success.

Music Producers of the United States (US):

Aftermath Records
2220 Colorado Blvd.
Santa Monica CA, 90404
Phone: 310 865 7642 Fax: 310 865 7068
www.aftermathmusic.com
Credits: Dr. Dre, Ice Cube Eminem, Snoop Dogg, Nas

AAM Management
7 West 22nd Street 4th Floor
New York, NY 10010
Phone: 212 924 2929 Fax: 212 929 6305
info@aaminc.com
Contact: Andy Kipnes, Paul Ebersold, Jerry Finn, William Orbit

Advanced Alternative Media
7 West 22nd Street, 4th Floor
NY 10010 New York
Phone: 212 924 2929
Contact: G.G. Garth
info@aaminc.com

BK Entertainment Group
15300 Ventura Blvd. Ste. 307
Sherman Oaks, CA 91403
Phone: 818 728 8200 Fax: 818 758 8213
reception@bkentertainmentgroup.com

Babyface/ Kenneth Edmonds
PO Box 877
Chaptaqua, NY 10514
Credits: Whitney Houston, Paula Abdul, Tony Braxton

Bad Boy Entertainment
1710 Broadway, 2nd Floor New York,
NY 10019
Phone: 212 381 1540 Fax: 212 381 1599
www.badboyonline.com
Contact: Nisan Stewart Sean Combs,
Ryan Leslie: Gniles@badboyworldwide.com

Bar Management
1501 Broadway, Suite 1914
New York NY 10046
Contact: Dame Grease
Credits: Fat Joe, DMX, N.O.R.E

Beatology Music
Web: www.myspace.com/beatology
Contact: Gordon McGinnis
Credits: Dr. Dre, 2 Pac, Snoop Dogg, Ice
Cube, George Clinton, Method Man, DMX, Mac Mall, Mack 10,
Kurupt

BJA Sound
New York, NY 10012
Phone: 917 406 9036
Email: info@bjasound.com
Contact: Ben Arrindell
Credits: Aretha Franklin, Busta Rhymes, K-Ci & Jo-Jo, 3LW, Mary J
Blige, Yolanda Adams

Chad Hugo

The Neptunes
1755 Broadway
New York NY 10019
Fax: 212 841 8099
www.startrakmusic.com
Credits: Clipse, Snoop Dogg, Brittany Spears, P Diddy

Chase Ent.

7378 West Atlantic Blvd #250
Margate, FL 33063
305 695 6731
www.chasent.net
mikeb@chasent.net
Contact: T-Pain, Jim Jonsin
Credits: Mike Jones, T-Pain

Cliff Brodsky

1865 Fuller Ave. Ste 212A
Hollywood, CA 90046
Email: cliff@brodskyentertainment.com
Credits: Universal, Sony, Interscope,
MCA

Craig Brockman

P.O. Box 571475
5550 Wilshire Blvd, Suite 301, Tarzana CA 91357
Phone 818 331 0544 Fax: 818 734 7282
www.hitclubentertainment.com
info@hitclubentertainment.com

C Management
13351-D Riverside Dr. Ste 275
Sherman Oaks Ca 91423
Phone: 818 990 3031 Fax: 818 990 3361
Email: claris@studioexpresso.com
Contact: Ken Allardyce, Rafa Sardina,
Credits: Green Day, Goo Goo Dolls, Avril Lavigne, Shakira, Beyonce

Das Communications
83 Riverside Drive, New York NY 10024
Phone: 212 877 0400 Fax: 212 595 0176
Contacts: Jerry Duplessis
Credits: Black Eyed Peas, Whitney Houston, Wyclef Jean,
Canibus, Fugees, Mya, Pras, Santana

Dragonman Entertainment
Pappelallee 88, 10437 Berlin Germany
Phone +49 30 443 286 11 Fax +49 30 443 286 12
www.dragonmanent.com
info@DragonManEnt.com
Contact: Taan Newjam/ Dragonman
Credits: Beenie Man, Britney Spears, Omarion, B2K

DJ Twinz
Ellis Entertainment/ James Ellis
900 South Ave, Suite 262
Staten Island, NY 10314
Phone: 718 568 3655 Fax: 718 568 3643
ellisentertain@aol.com
Credits: Redman

Grand Slam Ent.
4919 Murietta Ave
Sherman Oaks, CA 91423
Phone: 818 789 5964
Contact: Jeff Gordon
Credits: Toni Braxton, Madonna, Nappy Roots

Genuine Representation
11271 Ventura Blvd, Suite 225
Studio City, CA 91604
Phone: 818 505 6870 Fax: 818 505 6872
genuinerep@earthlink.net
Credits: Jay-Z, Kurupt, E-40, Nas, 50 Cent, Kelly Rowland, Destiny's Child, Will Smith, Tupac Shakur
Contact: Chris Johnson, Tim Riley, DJ Khaul, Rob Chiarelli, Brion James

Irv Gotti
825 8th Avenue 29th Floor
New York, NY 10019
Credits: Ashanti, DMX, Ja Rule, Jay-Z

Jermaine Dupri
So So Def
1350 Spring Street Suite 750, Atlanta GA 30309
www.sosodef.net
Credits: Da Brat, Bow Wow, Kris Kross

Jerry Wonder
Das Communications
83 Riverside Drive, New York, NY 10024
Phone: 212 877 0400 Fax: 212 595 0176
Credits: Canibus, Fugees, Mya, Santana, City High, Destiny's Child, Da Band, Wyclef Jean, Chingy, Ludacris

Just Blaze
127 West 26th Street Room 801
New York, NY 10001
Credits: Cam'Ron, DMX, Fabolous, Freeway, Mariah Carey, Memphis Bleek, Nelly, Snoop Dogg, Jadakiss, Jay-Z, Busta Rhymes, Beanie Sigel

Mannie Fresh
Cash Money Records
2800 Veterans Memorial Blvd, Metairie, La 70002
Fax: 504 835 3676
www.cashmoney-records.com

Michael Rafael
26030 Franklin Ln., Stevenson Ranch CA 91381
Email: earthtonesounds@hotmail.com

Matheo Prototype Ent.
1650 Ventura Broadway Ste 609, New York, NY 10109
Phone: 973-715-1101
Email: don@prototypeentertainment.com
Contact: Don DiNapoli
Credits: The Game

Michael Woodrum
Phone: 818-848-3393 Fax: 818 848 3344
Michael@woodrumproductions.com
Credits: Neptunes, Prince, Eric Clapton, Snoop Dogg

Brion James/ Genuine Music
11271 Ventura Blvd, Suite 225
Studio City, CA 91604
Phone: 818 505 6870 Fax: 818 505 6872
genuinerep@earthlink.net
Contact: Brion James
Justin Timberlake, Keith Sweat, Baby Face

Original Man Entertainment
545 8th Avenue, Suite 401, NY 10018 New York
Phone: 888 445 8708 Fax: 888 445 8708
omegllc@aol.com
Contact: Quest, Lace, Sean W. Banks, Sekou Branch, D/R Period, DJ
Rad, Miykal Snoddy
Credits: 50 Cent, Dru Hill, Pretty Ricky, Diplomats, 50 Cent

Quest
545 8th Avenue, Suite 401
New York NY 10018
Phone: 888 445 8708 Fax: 888 445 8708
Contact: Quest
Credits: 50 Cent

Ro Entertainment/ Banana Boat Studios
4007 West Magnolia Blvd
Burbank, CA 91505
Phone: 818 843 2628 Fax: 818 843 4480
Credits: Brandy, Dru Hill, Christina Aguilera

Rockwilder
Ellis Entertainment
900 South Ave, Suite 262, Staten Island, NY 10314
Phone: 718 568 3655 Fax: 718 568 3643
ellisentertain@aol.com
Contact: James Ellis
Credits: Redman, Fabolous, Fat Joe, Flipmode Squad, Jay-Z, Lil Kim,
Nas

Rodney Jerkins
Darkchild Entertainment, Inc.
PO Box 410
Pleasantville NJ, 08232
Credits: Jennifer Lopez

Sam Sneed
11271 Ventura Blvd, Suite 225
Studio City, CA 91604
Phone: 818 505 6870 Fax: 818 505 6872
genuinerep@earthlink.net
Credits: G-Unit, Jay-Z, Scarface, Snoop Dogg, Dr. Dre

Six Figga Entertainments
P.O. Box 2016, Fort Lee NJ 07024
Phone: 201 481 5229 Fax: 309 279 8818
www.sixfigga.com
digga@sixfigga.com
Contact: Darrell Branch
Credits: Jennifer Lopez, Jay Z, Cam'Ron

Swizz Beatz
Clear Vision Management
P.O. Box 3852
Alpharetta GA, 30023
andre@aaronsent.com
www.aaronsent.com
Credits: Jay-Z, Mary J. Blige, Limp Bizkit, DMX, Eve, Nas

Teamsta Entertainment
222 West 21st Street, Suite F311
Norfolk VA 23517
Phone: 757 435 5044
teamstaent@aol.com
Contact: Darryl Sloan, Dominic Lamb
Credits: Cassidy, G-Unit, Busta Rhymes

Team Lunatics
4246 Forest Park Avenue Suite 2C St.
Louis, MO 63108
Phone: 314 533 1155 Fax: 314 652 7319
Contact: Pimp Juice, Jason Epperson
Credits: Nelly

Tim Mosley
Beat Club
2220 Colorado Blvd
Santa Monica, CA 90404
Credits: Missy Elliott, Petey Pablo,
Bubba Sparxxx

Tim Anderson
651 271 0515 (Cell)
Email: tanderson2005@yahoo.com
Credits: House of Pain, Shaq, Snoop, Crazy Bone

Trak Starz Productions
PO Box 78804
St. Louis MO 63178
Credits: Chingy
Contact: Zo, Sham

Untouchables Entertainment Group
100 Piermont
Road Closter, NJ 07624
Phone: 201 767 6924 Fax: 201 784 3879
Contact: Edward Ferrell, Darren Lighty
Credits: Aaliyah, Next, 98 Degrees

Vachik Aghaniantz
Tel: 818 504 2065
Email: vachik.aghanintz@gmail.com
Credits: James Brown, Earth Wind and Fire, Crazy Bone, Ice T

WeninDoubt Productions
Marysville, California:
Contact: WeninDoubt
Credits- Ibu, Jargon, Jordan Segundo,
Jennifer hudson, E40, Lil Flip, Chamillionaire, Pretty Ricky

Worlds End
183 N. Martel Ave, Suite 270
Los Angeles, CA 90036
Phone: 323 965 1540 Fax: 323 965 1547
Contact: Tim Palmer, Steve Lillywhite,
Stephen Lironi, Marley Marl, Lou Giordano
Credits: Taking Back Sunday, Goo Goo Dolls, Kool G Rap, KRS-One,
LL Cool J, Pete Rock

Music Managers

Independent musicians such as performance artists, songwriters, and music producers should almost certainly employ an experienced manager. In fact, a music manager will most likely be the most important person in your career and the agreement you sign with that manager will be a significant factor for your business accomplishments.

The main responsibilities of your music manager are to develop, promote, and facilitate the business behind your career. This includes creating a professional package to shop your music around, booking shows, handling the financial, administrative and legal affairs such as publishing deals, recording, public relations, publicity, royalties, and music promotion. Music managers usually demand 15-20% of your gross income in exchange for their services. Below is a comprehensive list of some of the world's greatest music managers.

Music Managers of the United States (US):

Allure Media Entertainment
34 E. Germantown Pike, Suite 112
Norristown, PA 19401
215 601 1499
Contact: Casey Alrich
Genres: Hip-Hop, Pop, R&B

American Artists Entertainment Group
2106 79th Ct.
Vero Beach, FL 32966
Phone: 772 569 1040 Fax: 772 569 1051
Email: online@aaegec.com
Contact: Anthony Messina
Genres: Pop, R&B

Area 67 Management
2216 W. 103rd St., Cleveland, OH 44102
Phone: 216 235 4549 Fax: 216 939 8715
Contact: Jill Bandella
Genres: Hip-Hop, Pop, R&B, Rap,

Artistic Control
1350 Spring Street NW
Atlanta, GA 30309
Phone: 404-733-5511 Fax: 404-733-5512
Contact: Luci Raoof
Credits: Bow Wow, Da Brat, Jermaine Dupri, Chante Moore

A-Team Management
741 Piedmont Ave. Ste. 500
Atlanta GA 30308
Phone: 404 874 4016
www.myspace.com/dateamstars
ftsent1@aol.com
Contact: Chad Beatz, Alex Todd
Credits: Ashanti, David Banner, Jim Jones, Juvenile, Mario, Talib
Kweli

Aubrey Francis
Ready Or Not Productions
800 Huey P. Long Avenue
Gretna, LA 70053
Phone: 504 368 1029 Fax: 504 368 1999
Credits: Juvenile

Azoff Music Management
1100 Glendon Ave. Ste. 3000
Los Angeles, CA 90024
Phone: 310-209-3100 Fax: 310-209-3101
Email: susan.markheim@azoffmusic.com
Contact: Alison Azoff, Paul Geary, Irving Azoff, Susan Markheim,
John Baruck
Credits: Jewel, Baby Face, Christina Aguilera, DJ Quick, Back Street
Boys, Jodeci, Baby

BlackGround Entertainment
155 W 19th Street New York, NY 10011
Contact: Barry Hankerson
Credits: Aaliyah, R Kelly
Genre: Urban

Blacksmith Management
59 Maiden Lane 27th floor, New York NY 10038
Phone: 212 586 2112 Fax: 212 586 2116
Email: blacksmithmusic@gmail.com
Contact: Corey Smyth
Genre: Urban

Bliss Artist Management
P.O. Box 5011, Laurel, MD 20726
Phone: 301 938 0838 Fax: 888 608 5936
Email: bliss51@onebox.com
Contact: Linda Sharpless
Genre: Urban, Gospel, Rock, Blues, Hip Hop, Jazz

Big Noise
11 S. Angell St. Ste. 336, Providence, RI 02906
Phone: 401 274 4770
Email: al@bignoisenow.com
Contact: Al Gomes
Clients: Christina Aguilera
Genre: Pop, R&B, Jazz

Blast Management
Los Angeles, CA
Phone: 323 857 7299
Email: blastmusic1@yahoo.com
Contact: Aaron D. Jacoves
Genre: Manages Producers, Songwriters, TV, film, composers

BME
2144 Hills Avenue Suite D2, Atlanta GA 30318
www.bmerecordings.com
marmstrong@bmerecordings.com
Contacts: Lil Jon, Ron Mcdowell
Credits: Lil Jon & The East Side Boyz
Genre: Hip Hop

Borman Entertainment
1250 Sixth St. Ste. 401, Santa Monica, CA 90401
Phone: 310-656-3150 Fax: 310-656-3160
Email: bormanent@bormanla.com
Contact: Gary Borman, Ellynne Citron, Steve Moir, Barbara Rose
Credits: Faith Hill, Lone Star, Keith Urban, James Taylor, Garbage
Genre: Pop, Hip Hop

Brent Music Management
14431 Ventura Blvd. #306
Sherman Oaks, Ca 91423
Contact: Bobby Brent, Elysia Skye, Tom Peterson
Genre: Pop, Hip Hop, All Genres

Bullet Proof Music Management
PO Box 3239
CA, 93011 Camarillo
Phone: 805 815 7744
hitmusicman@yahoo.com
Contact: Ian Gold
Credits: Nicole Lacy
Genre: Dance, Pop

The Brokaw Company
9255 Sunset Blvd. Ste. 804
Los Angeles, CA 90069
Phone: 310-273-2060 Fax: 310-276-4037
Email: brokawc@aol.com
Contact: Joel Brokaw, David Brokaw
Credits: Tony Braxton, Michael Bolton, Kool & the Gang
Genre: Pop, Hip Hop

Caliente Entertainment
9348 Civic Center Dr. Mezzanine Level
Beverly Hills, CA 90210
Contact: Caresse Henry,
Artists: Madonna, Jessica Simpson, Joss Stone, Ricky Martin
Genre: Pop, Hip Hop

Carline Balan/ Balan Inc. Agency
21 West 58th St.
New York, NY 10019
Phone: 212 333 3522 Fax: 212 572 9839
Credits Jay-Z
Genre: Hip Hop

Chris Smith
Chris Smith Management
21 Camden St. 5th Floor
M5V 1V2 Toronto, Ontario Canada
Phone: 416-362-7771 Fax 416-362-6648
info@chrissmithmanagement.com
Contacts: Mandy Maguire
Credits: Nelly Furtado
Contact: Mandy Maguire, Chris Smith, Brian West, Gerald Eaton
Genre: R&B, Pop

Coast To Coast Music
P.O. Box 18334, Encino, CA 91416
Phone: 818 376 1380

Email: ccmusic@pacbell.net
Contact: Chris Fletcher
Genres: All

Countdown Entertainment
110 West 26th St. 3rd Floor
New York, NY 10001
Phone: 212 645 3068
james@countdownentertainment.com
Contact: James Citkovic
Genres: Country, Hip-Hop, Pop, Rock, R&B

Creative Management
3815 Hughes Avenue 3rd Floor
Culver City, CA 90232 USA
Phone: 310 841 4360
Contact: Kenneth Crear
Credits: 112, Nick Carter, Sisqo
Genre: R&B, Pop

Dalville Entertainment
4090 Concordia Way
Va Beach VA 23453
Phone: 757 362 2850
Email: Daville@verizon.net
Contact: Myron "Ron" Campbell
Credits: Tyrese, Brandy
Genre: Hip Hop, Pop, Urban

Dalville Entertainment (NY)
550 J Grand St #GC
NY 10002 New York
Phone: 347 653 1070
Contact: Anthony Gonzalez, Jr.
www.myspace.com/davillemanagement
Email: kingpaze@gmail.com
Genre: Hip Hop,Pop, Urban

David Lombard Management
P.O. Box 252, Hollywood CA 90078
Phone: 310-887-3972
davidlombardmgt@aol.com
Contact: David Lombard
Artists: Eric Benet, Johnny Gill, En Vogue
Genre: R&B, Jazz, Pop,

Def Ro Inc.
33 Prospect St. Ste 1R
Bloomfield, NJ 07003
Contact: Ro Smith
Clients: Mary J Blige
Genre: Hip Hop, R&B, Pop

Double Xxposure
West 34th St. Suite 201, New York NY 10016
Phone: 212 757 2669 Fax: 212 629 9410
Contact: Angelo Ellerbee
Credits: Lumidee
Genre: Hip Hop, R&B

Debbie Fontaine
Fontaine Music
11669 Santa Monica Blvd. Ste 202
Los Angeles, CA 90025 Fax: 310 471 8630
www.fontainetalent.com
info@fontainetalent.com
Genre: Hip Hop/Pop

Ebony Son Management
1867 7th Avenue Suite 4C
New York, NY 10026 Fax: 212 665 5197
Contact: Jeff Dixon, Chaka Zulu
jdixon914@aol.com
Credits: Chingy, Ludacris
Genre: Hip Hop

Ed Holmes Management
1775 Broadway Suite 2300, New York, NY 10019
Contact: Ed Holmes
Artists: Mase, Amerie
Genre: Hip Hop

Fresh Flava Entertainment
2705 12th St. NE
Washington, DC 20018
Phone: 202 832 7979 Fax: 202 635 0664
Email: freshflava1@aol.com
Contact: Emanuel Yeoman
Clients: Hush
Genre: Hip Hop, Jazz, Gospel, R&B, Rock

Fuse Entertainment
130 Church St. Ste. 166
New York, NY 10007
Fax: 212 812 5432
Contact: Don Desalvo
Genre: Hip Hop, Soul, Gospel, R&B, Club, House

Fuzed Music
P.O. Box 19436, Seattle WA 98109
Phone: 206 352 6892 Fax: 206 374 2429
Email: info@fuzedmusic.com
Contact: Grady Chapman
Genre: Hip Hop

✓ **Gee Roberson**
1290 Avenue of the Americas 27th Floor
New York NY 10104
Phone: 212 707 2000 Fax: 212 581 6414
www.atlantic-records.com
G.roberson@atlanticrecords.com
Credits: Kanye West, Lil Wayne, T.I.
Genre: Pop, Hip Hop

✓ **Grand Hustle Ent**
PMB 161541 10th Street
Atlanta GA 30318
www.grandhustle.com
Contact: Jason Geter
Credits: T.I.
Genre: Hip Hop

Greg Lyon
P.O. Box 881755, LA, CA 90009
Phone: 281 831 7629 Fax: 310 578 5977
Credits: Master P, Lil Romeo, Silkk, The Shocker
Genre: Hip Hop, R&B

✓ **Goliath Artists**
270 Lafayette St.
New York, NY 10012-3311
Phone: 212 324 2410
Contact: Paul Rosenberg
Credits: Eminem, Cypress Hill
Genre: Rap, Hip Hop

Graphite Media
1504 Bay Road #2409
The Flamingo
FL 33139 Miami Beach
Phone: 786 210 2369
Email: ben@graphitemedia.net
Contact: Ben Turner/ Music Manager

Headline Talent
1650 Broadway Ste. 508
New York NY 10019
Phone: 212 581 6900 Fax: 212 581 6906
Email: glknight10@yahoo.com
Genre: Hip Hop, Classic Rock

Hoffman Entertainment
362 5th Ave Ste 804
NY New York 10001
Phone: 212 765 2525
Fax: 212 765 2888
Hoffmanentertainment.com
Contact: Randy Hoffman
Credits: Thalia, Jessica Simpson
Genre: Pop, R&B

Intelligent Music
250 West. 57th Street Suite #2331
New York NY 10107
Phone: 212 262 1103 Fax: 212 262 1173
Email: bcelestin@nyct.net
Contact: Bob Celestin
Credits: Jodeci
Genre: R&B

James Ellis
Ellis Entertainment
900 South Avenue Suite 262
Staten Island, NY 10314
Phone: 718 568 3655 Fax: 718 568 3643
Email: ellisentertain@aol.com
Credits: Keith Murray, Redman
Genre: Hip Hop

KBM
1459 Morton Place
Los Angeles, CA 90026
Phone: 310-234-0280 Fax: 310-234-0282
Email: kbmgt@aol.com
Contact: Brent Harris
Artists: Tony, Toni, Tone, Sounds of Blackness, Rachelle Ferrell, Robin
Genre: Pop, Hip Hop

Lindsay Scott
8899 Beverly Blvd
Suite 600
Los Angeles, CA 90048
Phone: 310 860 1040 Fax: 310 860 1042
Credits: Pink, Janet Jackson
All Genres

Marquee Management
274 Madison Avenue
NY 10016 New York
Phone: 212 889 0420
Fax: 212 889 0279
Contact: Steven Kurtz
Credits: Christina Aguilera
Genre: Pop, Urban

Mad Management
5355 Cartwright Ave. Ste. 115
North Hollywood CA 91601
Phone: 323 908 1970
Email: Michael@madmanage.com
Contact: Michael Dutcher
Genres: Hip-Hop,, R&B, Jazz, Blues Alt

Major Production
330 East Maple Rd. Ste. 331
Birmingham, MI 48009
Phone: 248 647 2020
Email: major@themajorgroup.com
Contact: Brian Major
Genre: Rap, Jazz, Techno, Rock, Pop, R&B

Mickey Bentson
Pay Up Management
123 Pochin Place
Hampton, VA 23661

Credits: Ice-T, Amil, Fat Joe,
Contact: Mickey Bentson
Genre: Pop, Hip Hop

Mahogany Ent.
PO Box 4367
Mitchelville MD 20775
Phone: 301 390 8408 Fax: 301 390 9594
Contact: Shiba Freeman Haley
www.mahoganyinc.com
mahoganyinc@comcast.net
Genre: Urban

Million Dollar Artists
13001 Dieterle Lane
St. Louis, MO 63127
Phone: 314 965 5648
Email: maxmillion@milliondollarartists.net
Contact: Charles Million
All Genres

Nexus Management Group
430 W. 14th Street
NY 10014 New York
Phone: 212 929 3339 Fax: 212 937 2035
Contact: Ceci Kurzman
Credits: Shakira
Genre: Pop, Urban

Notable Entertainment
100-10A Dreiser Loop, NY 10475 Bronx
Contact: Linda Berk
Credits: Ashanti
Genre: Urban

✓ **Paul Rosenberg**
Goliath Artists
151 Lafayette Street, New York, NY 10013
Phone: 212 324 2410 Fax: 212 324 2415
Credits: Eminem, Xzibit, Cypress Hill
Genre: Hip Hop

✓ **Phil Robinson/Bad Boy**
1710 Broadway, New York NY 10019
Phone: 212 381 1540 Fax: 212 381 1599
Other Locations
1440 Broadway 16th Floor, New York, NY 10018
Credits: P. Diddy
Genre: Hip Hop, R&B

Powerblast Worldwide
15663 S.W. 41st ST.
Miami FL 33027
Phone: 305 335 2529
Contact: Ernest W. Coleman
Genre: Hip Hop, Reggae, R&B, Soul

Ron Robinson
Murder Management
825 8th Avenue 29th Floor, New York, NY 10019
Credits: Ja Rule
Genre: Hip Hop

Shiba Freeman Haley
Mahogany Entertainment
PO Box 4367, Mitchelville, MD 20775
Phone: 301 390 8408 Fax: 301 390 9594
www.mahoganyinc.com
Email: mahoganyinc@comcast.net
Credits: Yolanda Adams
Genre: Hip Hop

Simon Renshaw Strategic Artist Management
1100 Glendon Ave. Suite 1000
Los Angeles, CA 90024
Phone: 310 208 7882 Fax: 310 208 7881
Credits: Dixie Chicks, Cyndi Thomson
Jennifer Lopez, Clay Aiken,
Genre: Hip Hop, Pop

Soulicious Entertainment
PO Box 244
Elmwood Park NJ 07407
Phone: 201 398 0198 Fax: 201 398 1192
www.soulicious.com
Email: sbeeler@soulicious.com
Contact: Sam Beeler

Sorkin Productions
3742 Jasmine Ave. Suite 201
Los Angeles CA 90034
Phone: 310 559 5580 Fax: 310 559 5581
Contact: Don Sorkin
Genre: R&B, Dance, Rock, Pop

T-Bones Records
P.O. Box 46793
CA 90046 West Hollywood
Phone: 818 200 3221
www.tbonesrecords.com
Email: headfridge@socal.rr.com
Contact: Tim Ramenofsky
Credits: Afroman
Genre: Urban

Terror Squad Ent.
288 East 189th Street
Brooklyn, NY 10629
Email: flexts@aol.com
Contact: Flex
Credits Fat Joe
Genre: Hip Hop

Troy Carter
Erving Wonder Management
9255 Sunset Blvd. suite 200
LA, CA 90069
Phone: 323 461 1144 Fax: 310 205 5001
Email: troycarter@ervingwonder.com
www.ervingwonder.com
Credits: Freeway, Eve
Genre: Hip Hop

Turner Management
374 Poli St. Ste 205
Ventura CA 93001
info@turnermanagementgroup.com
Contact: Dennis Turner
Artists: Kenny G
Genre: Hip Hop, Pop, R&B

Violator Management
36 West 25th Street
11th Floor
New York, NY 10010
Phone: 646 486 8900 Fax: 646 486 8929
www.violator.com
Contact: Mona Scott, Chris Lighty, James Cruz, Claudine Joseph,
Andre Neal
Credits: 50 Cent, Tweet, Lil Mo, Missy Elliott, Macy Gray

Vision Entertainment Group
8484 Wilshire Boulevard Suite 425
CA, 90211 Beverly Hills
Phone: 323 951 9595 Fax: 323 951 9898
Contact: Andy Gould, Dan Dalton
Credits: Damian Marley, Jurassic 5, Stephen Marley
Genre: Country, Rock, Urban

Ronald Williams
Big Money Management
PO Box 547
Saint Rose, LA 70087
Fax: 504 466 7575
Credits: Big Tymers, Hot Boys, Juvenile, Lil Wayne
Genre: Hip Hop

Bryan Williams
Big Money Management
PO Box 547
Saint Rose, LA 70087
Fax: 504 466 7575
Credits: Big Tymers, Hot Boys, Juvenile
Lil Wayne
Genre: Hip Hop

Michele Williams
Big Cat Management
461 Leslie Street
Newark, NJ 07112
Phone: 908 339 2090
Fax: 973 282 0638
Credits: 3LW
Genre: Hip Hop

Wright Entertainment Group
424 East Central Blvd #189. Suite 500
Orlando, FL 32801
Phone: 407 826 9100 ext 182 Fax: 407 826 9107
www.wegmusic.com
Contact: Melinda Bell
Credits: Britney Spears, Backstreet Boys
Justin Timberlake, Nsync, Akon
Contact: Johnny Wright
Genre: Pop, Hip Hop

Yolanda Adams
N-House Management
P.O. Box 421476
Suite 220, West University
TX 77242 Houston
Phone: 281 531 0776 Fax: 281 531 0744
Email: info@nhousemanagement.com
Contact: Shiba Freeman Haley
Credits: Yolanda Adams
Genre: Urban

2 Deep Entertainment
P.O. Box 20097
New York, NY 10001
Email: info@2deepentertainment.com
Contact: Frankie Davis
Genre: R&B, Rap, Gospel, Pop

Music Managers of the United Kingdom (UK):

All Our Daze
0207 193 3560
www.allourdaze.com
info@allourdaze.com

Bionic Artists
Gavin Davies
63 Gifford Close, 2 Locks, NP44 7NY
07816 310 525
www.bionic-artists.com
gavin@bionic-artists.com

Elite Music Management
PO Box 3261, Brighton, BN2 4WA, UK.
01273 55 40 22
www.elitemm.com
hq@elitemm.com

Excession: The Agency LTD London UK
Claire Boyle
Unit 117, Westbourne Studios,
242 Acklam Road, London, W10 5JJ.
0207 524 7676
www.excession.co.uk
Claire@excession.co.uk

Ideal
Sacha Ideal
PO Box 191,
Benfleet, Essex, SS7 9FB
01268 796 120
01268 796 120
www.ideasdjs.co.uk

Jason Young
24 Thornberry, Letterkenny,
Co.Donegal, Ireland
0033 3879 660 222
www.jasonyoung.dj
info@jasonyoung.dj

Radius Music Management
Ben King
Office 1E, Bannon Court,
54-58 Michael Road, London, SW6 2EF.
0207 384 0555
www.radiusartists.com
ben@radiusartists.com

Safehouse Management
Lynn Cosgrave
PO Box 47200,
Lonodn, W6 6DQ
0208 743 4000
www.safehousemanagment.com
info@safehousemanagement.com

AIR
27 The Quadrangle,
49 Atalanta Street,
London, SW6 6TU.
0207 386 1600
0207 386 1619
www.airmtm.com
www.airmtm.com
jonny@airmtm.com

Anorak London
The Hood, 2nd Floor,
61-63 Brick Lane,
London, E1 6QL
0207 650 7840
www.scruffybird.com
info@anoraklondon.com

Big Life
0207 554 2100
www.biglifemanagement.com
colin@biglifemanagement.com

Carpe Diem
www.myspace.com/carpediemartistmanagement
Cdam07@gmail.com
Savage.entertainmentagency@yahoo.co.uk

CMO Management Int. LTD
Studio 2.6, Shepherds East,
Richmond Way, London, W14 0DQ.
0207 316 6969
0207 316 6970
www.cmomanagement.co.uk
CMOinfo@cmomanagement.co.uk

Convert Music
07958958541
www.convertmusic.co.uk
simon@convertmusic.co.uk

CEC Management
1st Floor, 65-69 White Lion Street,
London, N1 9PP
www.myspace.com/cecmanagementmusic
Char Evans—char@cecmanagement.com

Coalition Management
www.myspace.com/coalition
timvigon@mac.com/tp@coalitiongroup.co.uk

Crown Music Management
0207 371 5444
www.crownmusic.co.uk
info@crownmusic.co.uk

Crusin Music
PO Box 3187, Radstock, BA3 5WD
01373 834 161
www.crusin.co.uk
sil@crusin.co.uk/al@crusin.co.uk/louie@crusin.co.uk

Emperor Management
www.myspace.com/emperormanagement
John.empson@btopenworld.com

Empire Artist Management
Portobello Dock, 553-579 Harrow Road,
London, W10 4RH
0208 968 5888
www.empire-management.co.uk
info@empire-management.co.uk

Factory Music
216 Cherlton High Street,
Folkestone, Kent, CT19 4HS.
01303 274 189
www.factorymusic.co.uk
steve@factorymusic.co.uk/sharon@factorymusic.co.uk

Fredag
53 George IV Bridge,
Edinburgh, EH1 1EJ
0131 225 5522
talent@fredagartistgroup.com

Freshwater Hughes Management
PO Box 54 Northaw,
Herts, EN 4PY
01707 664 141
www.freshwaterhughes.com
info@freshwaterhughes.com

Goo Music
14 Hadley Grove,
Barnet, EN5 4PH
www.goomusic.net

Graphite Media
Graphite Media Limited,
133 Kew Road, Richmond,
TW9 2PN.
0208 948 5446
www.graphitemedia.net
info@graphitemedia.net

H360
www.myspace.com/simonrugg
simon@h360.co.uk

In Phase management
www.inphasemanagement.com
info@inpahsemanagement.com

JPR Management
PO Box 3062, Brighton, BN50 9EA
01273 779 944
www.jprmanagement.co.uk
info@jprmanagement.co.uk

Grenade Artist Management
www.myspace.com/grenadeartistmanagement
info@grenadearartists.com

IE Music
www.iemusic.co.uk

Native Management
32 Ransomes Dock,
35-37 Parkgate Road, SW11 4NP
0207 801 1919
www.nativemanagement.com
info@nativemanagement.com

Nettwerk Management UK
59-65 Worship Street,
London, EC2A 2DU
0207 456 9500
www.nettwerk.com
contactmanagement@nettwerk.com

Outside Management
Butler House,
177-178 Tottenham Court Road,
London, W1T 7NY
0207 436 3633
www.outside-org.co.uk
info@outside-org.co.uk

Out There Management
120—124 Curtain Road,
London, EC2 3SQ
0207 739 6903
mark@outthere.co.uk

P3 Music
www.p3music.com

Reverb XL
Reverb House, Bennett Street,
London, w4 2AH
0208 747 0660
www.reverbxl.com
management@reverbxl.com

Riverman Management
George House, Brecon Road,
London, W6 8PY
0207 381 4000
www.riverman.co.uk
info@riverman.co.uk

Rock Artist Management
Rothery House,
Henthorn Road,
Clitheore, BB7 2LD
01200 444 544
www.rockartistmanagement.com

Push Zero
Edinburgh, Scotland
mike@pushzero.co.uk
www.myspace.com/pushzero

Running Media Group
14 Victoria Road, Douglas,
Isle of Man, IM2 4ER
01624 677 214
www.runningmedia.com
management@runningmedia.com

Supervision Management
www.myspace.com/supervisionmanagement
info@supervisionmgt.com

The TCB Group
24 Kimberly Court, Kimberly Road,
Queens Park, London, NW6 7SL
0207 328 7272
www.tcbgroup.co.uk
info@tcbgroup.co.uk

TRC Management
10c Whit Court, Manor Park,
Manor Farm Road, Runcorn,
Cheshire, WA7 1TE
01928 571 111
www.trcmanagement.com
mail@trcmanagment.com

RWD
Danny Walker
Unit 2.1, Lafone House,
11-13 Leathermarket Street,
London, SE1 3HN, UK
08707 745 619
editor@rwdmag.com
www.Rwdmag.com

DJ Magazine
Martin Carvell
91 Brick Lane,
London, E1 6QL, UK.
0207 247 8855
editors@djmag.com
www.djmag.com

Music Publishers

A music publisher's business revolves around promoting, exploiting, and administrating the copyright in musical works. There are numerous ways in which you can use a music publisher to exploit your music. If your are planning to set up your own publishing business, an important source of income for your company will be generated from musical compositions and lyrics. This includes performance rights, synchronization licenses, and mechanical licenses. It has been proven that nearly every independent publisher has subcontracted their musical content to an established and experienced publisher who has the infrastructure to exploit the musical works on a major scale.

Usually in a sub-publishing agreement, you, the independent publisher, will have 100% copyright ownership to begin with. You then subcontract a specific publisher to exploit your content based on the agreed terms and conditions between both publishers. The profit split is more often than not 50/50. However, it is common for the independent publisher to demand a 75/25 split on the returns. It is best practice to seek professional legal advice from a music or entertainment lawyer before making deals in which you give others a share of you copyrights for your content. Below is a list of reputable publishers you could send your musical works to for sub- or co-publishing deals.

Music Publishers of the United States (US):

Alva Music Publishing
P.O. Box T / 16311 Askin Dr.
Pine Mountain Club, CA 93222
Phone: 661 242 0125 Fax: 661 242 8334
Contact: Eddie Gurren
Accepts Unsolicited Material

Arthouse Entertainment
2324 El Contento Drive
Los Angeles CA, 90068
Phone: 323 461 3400 Fax: 323 375 0490
www.arthouseent.com
Stephen@ArtHouseEnt.com
Contact: Stephen J Finfer
Credits: Snoop Dogg

Abet Music
1938 S. Myrtle Ave.
Monrovia, CA 91016
Phone: 626 303 4114 Fax: 626 205 3879
Email: tony@abetmusic.com
Contact: Tony Nersoya

Avatardigi Digital Distribution
2029 hyperion avenue
Los Angeles, ca 90027
Phone: 323 906 1500
Contact: Lynnette Jenkins
Credits: Boys II Men, Ja Rule, Guy, Vinx, Planet Asia, Keith Murray, Tony Toni Tone, DMX, Brandy, Tupac, Redman, Foxy Brown, Spice 1, Vanessa Williams, Bell Biv Devoe, Patti Labelle, One Block Radius

Big Fish Music
12720 Burbank Blvd.
Valley Village, CA 91607
Phone: 818 508 9777
Clisag21@yahoo.com
Contact: Chuck Tennin, Lora Sprague
All Genres

Blast Music Publishing
P.O. Box 40027
Fort Worth TX 76140
Phone: 817 595 6955 Fax: 817 887 2555
blastmusiq@sbcglobal.net
Contact: Steve Blast
Credits: Nelly, Chingy
Genre: Hip Hop, R&B

BMG Music Publishing
8750 Wilshire Blvd.
Beverly Hills, CA 90211
www.bmgmusicsearch.com
Contact: Elizabeth Brooks
Artists: Maroon 5, Beck, Cold Play, Nelly, Christina Aguilara, All-American Rejects, Chad Hugo, Chingy
All Genres

BMG Music Publishing
1540 Broadway 39th Floor.
New York, NY 10036
Contact: Adam Epstein
www.bmgmusicsearch.com
Artists: Beck, Cold Play, Nelly, Erykah Badu, Cypress Hill, The Cure, BB-King, Chingy
All Genres

BMG Music Publishing
1400 18th Avenue South
Nashville TN 37212
www.bmgmusicsearch.com
Contact: Michelle Berlin/ Country
All Genres

BMI
8730 Sunset Blvd. 3rd Floor
West Hollywood CA 90069
Phone: 310 659-9109 Fax: 310 657 6947
Email: losangeles@bmi.com
All Genres

Breakthrough Creations
514 Laurel Grove Circle, Santa Rosa, CA 95407
Phone: 415 898 0027 Fax: 415 898 1104
Contact: Sam Watters
Credits: Jessica Simpson
Genre: Pop

Bubo Music
1251 W. Sepulveda Blvd Suite 107, Torrance CA 90502
Phone: 310 544 9462
varicksmith3892@yahoo.com
Contact: Varick D. Smith
Credits: Beyoncé
Genre: Hip Hop, R&B

Damon Sharpe Music
15030 Ventura Blvd. Suite 19—716
Sherman Oaks CA 91406
Phone: 818 505 6870 Fax: 818 505 6872
www.damonsharpe.com
info@damonsharpe.com
Contact: Damon Sharpe
Genre: Urban, Pop

Double Xxposure

846 7th Ave. 2nd Floor

New York NY 10019

Phone: 212 757 2669 Fax: 212 445 0941

Contact: Angelo Ellerbee

Credits: DMX

Genre: Hip Hop, R&B

Eddie Ferrell (Eddie Music)

100 Piermont Road

Closter, NJ 07624

Phone: 201 767 6924 Fax: 201 784 3879

Credits Ruff Endz

Genre: Hip Hop, R&B

Ej Gurren Music

P.O. Box T / 16311 Askin Drive

Pine Mountain Club, CA 93222

gbrmusic@frazmtn.com

Contact: Eddie Gurren

Genre: R&B, Hip Hop, Gospel

EMI Music Publishing

2700 Colorado Ave. Ste. 100

Santa Monica, CA 90404

Phone: 310-586-2700 Fax: 310-586-2758

www.emimusicpub.com

Credits: Alicia Keys, The Neptunes, Usher, Jay-Z, Jermaine Dupri, Rodney Jerkins, Ludacris, Kandi,

Genre: Pop, Hip Hop

Famous Music

10635 Santa Monica Blvd. Ste 300

Los Angeles CA 90025

Phone: 310 441 1312 Fax: 310 441 4722

Contact: Carol Spencer, Maya Futrell

Credits: Bjork, 3LW

Flattime Records
5536 Wainwright Dr.
Fort Worth TX 76112
Phone: 818 239 9101 Fax: 817 887 3637
phlhwk9@aol.com
Contact: Phillip Hawkins
Genre: Dance / Pop / Urban

Hitco Music Publishing
500 Bishop St. NW STE A4
Atlanta GA 30318
c.simmons@hitcomusic.com
Genre: Urban

House Of Fame
118 16th Ave S. Ste 203
Nashville TN 37203
Contact: Mark Hall
Genre: Country, R&B, Soul

Lake Transfer Music
11300 Hartland St.
N. Hollywood CA 91605
Phone: 818 508 7158
Contact: Tina Antione
Genre: Pop, Hip Hop, R&B, Rock, Dance

Marc Anthony Publishing
591 Broadway Suite 3A
New York NY 10012
Phone: 212 274 0095 Fax: 212 274 9498
Contact: Jennifer Nieman
Credits: Marc Anthony
Genre: Pop

Mudslide Music
6607 Sunset Blvd.
Los Angeles CA 90028
Phone: 323 465 2700
Contact: Rick Ross
Genre: Hip hop, Reggae, Rock

Notation Music Publishing
7 Pratt Blvd. Glen Cove, NY 11542
Phone: 516 759 7550 Fax: 516 759 3113
Contact: Ric Wake, Jane Young
Genre: Pop, R&B

Paradise Forever Music
PO Box 170380 North Shore Branch
Glendale WI 53217
Phone 414 248 0759
pforevermusic@aol.com
Contact: Gerald Williamson
Genre: Pop/ Urban

Quincy Jones Music Publishing
6671 Sunset Blvd. # 1574A
Los Angeles, CA 90028
Phone: 323-957-6601 Fax: 323-962-5231
Contact: Marc Cazorla
www.quincyjonesmusic.com
info@quincyjonesmusic.com
Genre: Pop, Hip Hop

Real Songs Publishing
6363 Sunset Boulevard 8th Floor
Los Angeles CA 90028
Phone: 323 462 1709
Fax: 323 462 1713
Contact: Dianne Warren

Rondor Music International Inc.
2440 Sepulveda Blvd. Ste. 119
Los Angeles CA 90064
Phone: 310-235-4800
Email: Rondoria@umusic.com
Artists: Avril Lavigne, Obie Trice, Bobby Valentino and Twista

Rosen Music Corp
2021 Westgate Avenue
Los Angeles CA 90025
Phone: 310 230 6040 Fax: 310 230 4074
www.rosenmusiccorp.com
steven@rosenmusiccorp.com
Contact: Steven Rosen
Credits: Brandy, Christina Aguilera Dru Hill

The Royalty Network, Inc.
12650 Riverside Dr. Ste 203
Valley Village, Ca 91607
Phone: 818-762-0775 Fax: 818-762-1652
Contact: Steven C. Weber
Artists: Dead Prez, Muggs

Seedmusik Publishing
P.O. BOX 7076
Douglasville GA, 30154
Phone: 404 201 3551
www.seedmusik.com
seedmusik@yahoo.com
Contact: Kenye Waters
Genre: Urban

Silver Blue Music
3940 Laurel Canyon Blvd. Ste 441
Studio City, CA 91604
Phone: 818 980 9588 Fax: 818 980 9422
Contact: Joel Diamond

SONY/ATV MUSIC PUBLISHING LLC (Nashville)
8 Music Square West
TN 37203 Nashville
Phone: 615 726 8300 Fax: 615 726 8329
www.sonyatv.com
Contact: Troy Tomlinson: Troy_tomlinson@sonymusic.com

SONY/ATV
550 Madison Avenue
New York, NY 10022
Phone: 212 833 8000 Fax: 212 833 4742
www.sonyatv.com
Contact: Bill Brown, Rich Christina, Danny Strick

Ten Ten Music Group
33 Music Square W. Ste 110
Nashville, TN 37203
Phone: 615 255 9955 Fax: 615 255 1209
www.tentenmusic.com
All Genres

Transition Music
11288 Ventura Blvd. #709
Studio City, CA 91604
Phone: 323 860 7074 Fax: 323 860 7086
Contact: Jennifer Brown
All Genres (Especially music for TV and Film)

Universal Music Publishing
2440 Sepulveda Blvd. Ste. 100
Los Angeles, CA 90064
Phone: 310-235-4700 Fax: 310-235-4903
www.umusicpub.com
Contact: Tom Sturges, Donna Caseine
Artists: Anastacia, Ice Cube, Brian Mcknight, Montel Jordan, Outkast

Universal Music Publishing/ NY
1755 Broadway 8th floor
Rock, Country, Pop, Hip Hop
New York, NY 10019
Phone: 212-841-8156
www.umusicpub.com
Contact: Rebecca Wright,
Artists: 3 Doors Down, Outcast, Afro Man

Varry White Music/ Delicious Vinyl
6607 Sunset Blvd.
Los Angeles CA 90028
Phone: 323 465 2700
Contact: David Lyman, Karen Hogan
Genre: Hip Hop, Reggae, Rock

Warner Publishing
10585 Santa Monica Blvd. 3rd Floor
Los Angeles CA 90025
Phone: 310 441 8706 Fax: 310 470 3232
www.warnerchappell.com
Contact: Greg Sowders, Richard Blackstone
Credits: Green Day, Radiohead, Nickelback

Windswept Holding LLC
9320 Wilshire Blvd. Ste. 200
Beverly Hills, CA 90212
Phone: 310-550-1500 Fax: 310-247-0195
Contact: Debbie Dill,
www.windsweptpacific.com
ddill@windsweptpacific.com
Genre: Pop, Hip Hop

ZOMBA Music Publishing
137-139 West 25th Street 11th Floor
New York, NY 10001
Phone: 212 824 1249 Fax: 212 242 7462

Contact: David Mantel, Howie Abrams
Genre: R&B, Pop, Hip Hop
Music Publishers of the United Kingdom (UK):

Annie Reed
Little Shambles, 132 Top Lane,
Whitley, Wilt, SN12 8QY
01225 707 847
www.anniereedmusic.com
annie@anniereedmusic.com

BDI Music
Onward House, 11 Uxbridge Street,
London, W8 7TQ
0207 243 4101
www.bdimusic.com
info@bdimusic.com

Bucks Music Group
Onward House, 11 Uxbridge Street,
London, W8 7TQ
0207 221 4275
www.bucksmusicgroup.com
info@bucksmusicgroup.co.uk
Sony/ATV
30 Golden Square,
London, W1F 9LD
0203 206 2501
www.sonyatv.com
Ian.ramage@sonyat.com/flash.taylor@sonyatv.com
James.Dewar@sonyatv.com / brian.mahoney@sonyatv.com

Yell Music
PO Box 46301, London, W5 3UX
0208 579 8300
www.yellmusic.com
Jana.yell@yellmusic.com

Wardlaw Banks
Park House, 111 Uxbridge Road,
London, W5 5LB
0845 299 0150
www.wardlawnbanks.com

Gigging Venues & Promoters

Nightclub venue owners/managers have a need to keep their venues full as regularly as possible. Therefore, as a music and entertainment entrepreneur, you should take full advantage and seize the opportunity to satisfy the needs of these venues and club promoters to fill their venues with customers—your fans. Your goal is to exercise the proposal techniques mentioned in chapter seven to pitch your ideas to fill the venue with people thus giving you an opportunity to perform or promote your artist and earn some money at the same time. It is very important that you take into account that the way in which you approach these venue managers or club promoters will determine any positive decisions they make.

So get your presentation right and emphasize the benefits for them or their venues. Always approach them with the idea that you are doing something for them and not the other way round. Below is a comprehensive list of quality venues in the UK that you can do business with:

Venues & Promoters of the United Kingdom (UK)

....

12 Bar Club
Denmark Street, WC2H 8NL
www.12barclub.com
www.myspace.com/12barclub
12barclub@btconnect.com
Send demos and proposals to Andy Lowe

93 Feet East
Brick Lane, E1 6QL
www.93feeteast.co.uk
sean@93feeteast.co.uk
www.myspace.com/93feeteast

The Bird's Nest
Deptford Church Street, SE8 4RZ
www.myspace.com/deptfordbirdnest

The Bitter End
High Street,
Romford, RM1 1JU
www.myspace.com/thebitterenvenue

Borderline
Orange Yard, off Manette Street,
W1D 4AR.
www.mamagroup.co.uk/borderline
www.myspace.com/borderline

Bugbear Bookings
Dublin Castle, Parkway, Camden, NW1.
Hope & Anchor, Upper Street, Islington, N1.
www.bugbearbookings.com

Bullet Bar Promotions

Bullet Bar, Kentish Town Road, NW1 8PB.

www.myspace.com/bulletbarpromotions

Café Rocks

Café De Paris, Coventry Street, W1.

www.caferocks.co.uk

mickeyp@cafedeparis.co.uk

Chamber Music

The Windmill, Blenheim Gardens,

Brixton, SW2 5BZ

The Legion,

Old Street, EC1 9NQ

thisischamber@yahoo.co.uk

www.myspace.com/thisischamber

Communion

Notting Hill Arts Club,

Notting Hill Gate, W11 3LQ.

www.myspace.com/getcommunion

Corrupt Events/Casino Royale

Barfly, Chalk Farm Road, NW1

genia@corruptmanagement.com

www.myspace.com/corruptevents

Curious Generation

www.curiousgeneration.com

info@curiousgeneration.com

www.myspace.com/curiousgeneration

Dead or Alive
Punk, Bar Rumba,
The Comedy, The Buffalo,
The Last Days of Decadence,
The Famous Three Kings,
Acoustic Venue.
www.deadoralive.org.uk
www.myspace.com/dealoralivepromotions
gigs@deadoralive.org.uk

Dice Club
Hoxton Square
Bar and Kitchen,
Shoreditch, N1 6NU
www.myspace.com/diceclublondon

Elbow Promotions
The Fiddlers Elbow, 1 Malden Road,
Kentish Town, NW5 3HS.
Dan on 07877798233
www.myspace.com/elbowpromotions

Electro Acoustic Club
The Slaughtered Lamb (Clerkenwell)
The Luminaire (Kilburn)
Union Chapel (Islington)
www.electroacoustic.com
will@electroacousticclub.com
www.myspace.com/electroacousticclub

The Fighting Cocks
56 London Road, Kingston, KT2 6QA.
www.the-fighting-cocks.co.uk
www.myspace.com/thefightingcockkingston

Flag Promotions
www.flagpromotions.com
www.myspace.com/flagpromotions
Send demo CD to MySpace Submissions,
Flag Promotions, PO Box 181, Wembly, HA0 4BE and mention MySpace.

Fleur-De-Lys
The Lexington, The Slaughtered Lamb (Clerkenwell)
www.myspace.com/fleurdelyclub

The Gaff
382 Holloway Road,
London, N7 6PN
thegaffclublondon@live.co.uk
www.myspace.com/thegaffclub

The George Tavern
373 Commercial Road,
Stepney, E1 0LA
www.myspace.com/thegeorgetavern

Glasswerk
www.glasswerk.co.uk
www.myspace.com/glasswerkmusic

Goldmine
The Rhythm Factory,
16-18 Whitechapel Road,
London, E1 1EW
www.myspace.com/goldmineuk

Halfmoon Putney
The Halfmoon
93 Lower Richmond Road,
Putney, SW15 1EU
www.halfmoon.co.uk

Hardware
The Fighting Cocks,
56 London Road, Kingston KT2 6QA.
www.myspace.com/theoldkingsheadrocks

Hidden Away Music
Bertle's Bar, Downstairs from The Prince of Wales,
2 Hartfield Road,
Wimbledon, SW19 3TA
The Sapphire Lounge,
99 Buckingham Palace Road,
Victoria SW1! 0RP.
www.myspace.com/hiddenawaymusic

Jealous of the Daylight
The Old Queen's Head,
44 Essex Road, Islington, N1 8LN
www.myspace.com/jealousofthedaylight
jealousofthedaylight@gmail.com

Kaparte Promotions/Nocturne Folks
Bardens Boudoir, Temple Pier, Halfmoon (Herne Hill)
www.kaparte.info
events@kaparte.info

King Monkey Promotions
The Wilmington Arms,
60 Rosebury Avenue,
Clerkenwell, ECR 4RL
www.myspace.com/kingmonkeypromotions

Liar Liar Club
New Cross Inn,
323 New Cross Road,
London, SE14 6AS
www.myspace.com/liarliarclub

Monkey Boy Promotions
The Flag,
Station Road, Watford, WD17 1ET
www.myspace.com/monkeyboypromotions
monkeyboypromotions@hotmail.com

Monto Water Rats
The Water Rats,
327 Gray's Inn Road,
London, WC1X 8BZ
www.themonto.com

North South Divide
333 Mother,
333 Old Street, London, EC1V 9LE.
nsdgigs@yahoo.co.uk
www.myspace.com/northsouthdivide

Offline Club
The Prince Albert,
418 Coldharbour Lane,
Brixton, SW9 8LF
www.myspace.com/offlineclub

Rock 'n' Roll Cabaret
The Dublin Castel,
94 Parkway, Camden,
NW1 7AN
www.myspace.com/rockrollcabaret

Rough Trade Shops' Rota Afternoon
Notting Hill Arts Club,
Notting Hill Gate, W11 3JQ
www.myspace.com/rotaclub

South of the Border
350 Old Street, London, EC1C 9NQ.
www.myspace.com/southoftheborderrocks
www.myspace.com/kbyrocks

The Good Ship
289 Kilburn High Road.
Kilburn NW6 7JR
www.thegoodship.co.uk
john@thegooship.co.uk
Jessica@thegoodship.co.uk

The Luminaire
311 Kilburn High Road,
Kilburn, NW6 7JR
www.theluminaire.co.uk
bookings@theluminaire.co.uk
www.myspace.com/theluminaire

The Old Blue Last
38 Great Eastern Street,
Shoreditch, EC2A 3ES.
www.theoldbluelast.com
oldbluelast@vice.com
www.myspace.com/oldbluelast

This Is Music
www.myspace.com/thisismusiclondon
tiger@fourthfloormusic.com

Up All Night Promoters
20 Denmark Street,
Soho, WC2H 8NA
www.upallnightmusic.com
info@upallnightmusic.com
www.myspace.com/upallnightpromotions

What's Cookin
The Sheepwalk,
692 High Road, Leytonstone, E11
www.whatscookin.co.uk
ramblinsteve@whatscookin.co.uk

Windmill
22 Blenheim Gardens,
Brixton, SW2 5BZ
www.windmillbrixton.co.uk
windmillbrixton@yahoo.co.uk
www.myspace.com/windmillbrixton

Lofi Hifi
The Louisana,
Wapping Road, Bathurst Terrace,
Bristol, BS1 6UA
www.myspace.com/lofihifi

Offbeat Promotions
www.myspace.com/offbeatpromotions

The Fleece
12 St Thomas Street, Bristol, BS1 6JJ
www.fleecegigs.co.uk
dave@dcbpromotions.com
www.myspace.com/thefleecebristol

444 Club
The Rainbow,
160 High Street Deritend,
Digbeth, B12 0LD
www.myspace.com/kamokazeevents
bookings@kamikazeevents.com

10 Lives
The Flapper,
Cambiran Wharf, Kingston Row,
Birmingham, B1 2NU.
www.myspace.com/10livesmusicvenue

The Catapault Club
The Actress and Bishop, 35 Ludgate Hill,
Birmingham, B3 1EH
www.myspace.com/thecatapultclub

Cable Club
Prince Albert, 48 Trafalgar Street,
Brighton, BN1 4ED
www.myspace.com/cablclub
Send demos to address or to cableclub@hotmaill.com

Its Alive
Hectors House, Grand Parade,
Brighton, BN2 9QA
www.myspace.com/itsalivehectors
itsalive39@yahoo.com

Kong Promotions
www.kongpromotions.co.uk
info@kongpromotions.co.uk
www.myspace.com/kongpromo

Punker Bunker
Hobgonlin Pub, Engine Room, The Prince Albert
www.myspace.com/punkerbunker

Ranelagh Arms
The Ranelagh Arms,
2-3 High Street, Brighton, BN2 1RP
www.myspace.com/theranelagh
www.theranelagh.co.uk

Sound Factory
The Providence, 130 Western Road,
Hove, BN3 1DA
www.myspace.comprovuk

The Blub Bash
www.myspace.com/thebulbbash

The Gilded Palace of Sin
www.thegildedpalaceofsin.com
demoposse@theglidedpalaceofsin.com

The Hope
The Hope, 11-12 Queens Road,
Brighton, BN1 3WA
www.myspace.com/thehopevenue
thehope@drinkbrighton.co.uk

Bomb Ibiza
The Retro Bar, 78 Sackville Street,
Manchester, M1 3NJ
www.myspace.com/bombibiza

Designer Magazine
www.myspace.com/designermagazine

Eba Promotions
The Thirsty Scholar,
50 New Wakefield Street,
Manchester, M1 5NP
www.myspace.com/ebapromotions

Leaf Promotions
The Retro Bar,
78 Sackville Street,
Manchester, M1 3NJ
www.leafpromotions.co.uk

CPSIA information can be obtained at www.ICGtesting.com
Printed in the USA
LVOW04s0845030115

421340LV00003B/152/P

9 780956 650801